"MESSIANIC JUDAISM
IS NOT
CHRISTIANITY"

"MESSIANIC JUDAISM IS NOT CHRISTIANITY"

A LOVING CALL TO UNITY

STAN TELCHIN

Chosen
Grand Rapids, Michigan

Published by Chosen Books
A division of Baker Publishing Group
P. O. Box 6287, Grand Rapids, MI 49516-6287
www.chosenbooks.com

Printed in the United States of America

Library of Congress Cataloging-in-Publication Data
Telchin, Stan
    Messianic Judaism is not Christianity : a loving call to unity / Stan
Telchin.
        p.   cm.
    Includes bibliographical references.
    ISBN 0-8007-9372-2 (pbk.)
    1. Messianic Judaism—Controversial literature. 2. Judaism (Christian theology) I. Title.
    BR158.T45 2004
    289.9—dc22   2004009116

To my late wife, Ethel,
who understood
and is rejoicing in the presence of the Lord

and

to all who have ears to hear

CONTENTS

BEFORE YOU READ ON

A Note from the Author

When a friend of mine read the first draft of this book and suggested that I title it "*Messianic Judaism Is Not Christianity*," I was stunned. The statement seemed so harsh, so black or white. I was afraid it would offend my brothers and sisters in the Messianic movement. And the statement is false!

When I shared my reactions with him, he asked, "But isn't it true? Don't most of those in Messianic Judaism say that Messianic Judaism is not Christianity?"

I could not contradict him.

But their understanding should not be taken as a denial of their love for Jesus, the Messiah. Rather it is a reflection of the widespread misimpression that the words *Christian* and *Gentile* are synonymous. They are not. And some in Messianic Judaism—as well as in the Church—insist that you cannot be a Jew and a Christian at the same time! This assertion is false.

It is true that if one is a Jew, then he or she cannot be a Gentile. And if one is a Gentile, he or she cannot be a Jew. But you can certainly be a Jew and a Christian at the same time. This is what I am! And I maintain in this book that my Jewish brothers and sisters in the Messiah—that is to say, in Christ—are Christians and, according to Scripture, "one new man" with my Gentile brothers and sisters (see Ephesians 2:15).

I have written this book to reveal and to help heal the division that is occurring among brothers and sisters in the Messiah—a division being fostered by those who insist that Messianic Judaism is not Christianity.

FOREWORD

S tan Telchin is a Jew who loves being Jewish. He
also loves Jesus. And he believes that the most anti-
Semitic thing you can ever do to a Jewish person is
not to tell him about the Messiah.

Stan and I first met in 1975 just before he became
a follower of Jesus. Over the years we have stayed in
fairly close contact. Indeed, for eight years I served as a
member of the board of directors for Stan Telchin Ministries, Inc. So you can say with assurance that I know
him fairly well. You can also be sure that I admire him
and have profound respect for the way God has used
him over the years.

After coming to faith in Y'shua, he found a spiritual
home in one of the larger and more effective Messianic
congregations. For a time he was happy there and found
himself growing to understand and love Jesus. But he
was increasingly uneasy about a number of things he
observed. He was troubled by the fact that Jews who
came to faith in Jesus and who made their spiritual
homes in more conventional churches were regarded as
lesser brethren. He was also troubled by such terms as

Gentile Church when he knew that the Messiah established only one Church. In this book Stan will discuss these as well as other issues that have troubled him over the years.

After training for the ministry, Stan set out to establish the kind of congregation in which both Jews and Gentiles would feel at home and in which these problems would not be present. It was obvious to all that Stan and his first wife, Ethel (now in the presence of the Lord), were *very* Jewish. He did not feel he had to prove his Jewishness to anyone. And so he concentrated his efforts on teaching his congregation more and more about Jesus, on seeing their lives transformed and on helping them reach out to others.

What Stan will tell you in this book may come as a revelation. Certainly it will be controversial. Questions should arise and much discussion should be the result. I think this is what Stan had in mind when he decided—with difficulty—to write this book. I have often heard him say, "I am a lover and not a fighter." As you read on, I know Stan wants you to consider carefully what he has lovingly set forth.

That Stan Telchin loves Jews and that he wants to relate to Jews who believe in Jesus, even as he wants to relate to Gentile believers, will be clear to you as you read this book. Whether you agree or disagree with Stan, you need to hear what he is saying.

Moishe Rosen
Founder, Jews for Jesus

PREFACE

T wo thousand years ago the Jewish believers who were at the Jerusalem Council meeting described in Acts 15 asked an important question: "What must Gentiles do in order to become followers of Jesus, the Jewish Messiah?"

Today, two thousand years later, the opposite question is being asked: "What must Jews do in order to become followers of Jesus, the Jewish Messiah?"

Keep this question in mind as you consider what follows.

Please also recognize that while I am very closely associated with Jews for Jesus, the opinions I express in this book are mine. They are based upon my personal experiences and research and should not be construed to be the opinions of Jews for Jesus.

ACKNOWLEDGMENTS

I thank God for the opportunity He has given me to serve Him. I am grateful, too, for the way the eyes of my understanding have been opened as I have studied His Word.

Over the decades I have been blessed and challenged by the statements and writings of brothers in the faith who are on different sides of the issues addressed in this book—men like Arnold Fruchtenbaum, Dan Juster, Baruch Maoz, David Stern, Kai Kjaer-Hansen, the late Louis Goldberg, Michael Brown, John Fischer, William Varner, Arthur Glasser and many others.

I am grateful as well to Moishe Rosen, David Brickner and the wonderful men and women of Jews for Jesus who have truly blessed me. As I approached the age of 80, they had enough confidence in me to permit me to serve with them as a missionary. My admiration for them is great, and my commitment to the mission of our organization is complete: to make the Messiahship of Jesus an unavoidable issue to our Jewish people worldwide.

But as close as I am to Jews for Jesus, I must again state that the opinions I share in this book are mine and are not to be attributed to our ministry.

To the extent that I have erred in any way, I alone take full responsibility.

I cannot end this list of acknowledgments without also expressing my gratitude to two very special women. Jane Campbell, my editor at Chosen Books, insisted that I do this book and then inspired and encouraged me in the process. The other key woman is my wife, Elaine. Thank you, dear, for your encouragement, support and patience during the long days, weeks and months I spent working at my computer. You have really blessed me with your unconditional love and support.

And finally, I thank you, my reader, for taking the time to carefully consider this most important matter.

INTRODUCTION

Two amazing phenomena took place in 1967: Jerusalem was restored to Jewish hands for the first time in almost two thousand years, and Jewish people by the thousands started to come to faith in Jesus as their Messiah and Lord.

The first phenomenon has been fully explored by the media, but the second has not received the attention it deserves. It was as if Luke 21:24 was coming alive before our very eyes: "Jerusalem will be trampled on by the Gentiles until the times of the Gentiles are fulfilled." It was again time to bring the Gospel to the Jewish people.

But how was the Church to respond to the Jewish people who were coming to faith in Jesus? Should the Church today respond as the historical Church, which said, "Welcome into the Church. You are no longer Jews. You are now Christians"? Or should the Church recognize that Jewish identity is a matter of birth and a covenant relationship with God that goes all the way back to Abraham?

And how should new Jewish believers express their faith? Should they call themselves "Christians" and disappear into the "Church"? Weren't Christians the persecutors of the Jewish people? And wasn't the Church the place where that persecution was nurtured?

How were they to live as Jewish believers in Messiah Jesus? Should they form congregations of their own where they could remain Jews in lifestyle and practice and where they would be able to express their faith in a Jewish way?

Many felt that was precisely what they should do. They would not call themselves "Christians"; they would call themselves "Messianic Jews." And they would not call their meeting places "churches"; they would call them "Messianic congregations."

The changes seemed to work for both groups. Many in the Church would not have to worry about what to do with this strange, though richly endowed, people. And the Jewish believers would not expose themselves to more rejection and discomfort.

In appearance, aside from the absence of a cross and the presence of a menorah (the seven-branched candlestick representing the lampstand in the Temple), the Messianic congregation was like the early Church. Indeed, Christianity began as a congregational movement.

The services in these new congregations would be replete with Jewish flavor and expressions of Jewish culture in the hope that this emphasis would reach other Jewish people. And as more and more Jewish people came to faith, they hoped to be used by God to reach the entire Gentile world.

That was the hope. But what is the reality?

As the years passed, some in the movement felt that the congregations should be "more Jewish," and the way they chose to express their "Jewishness" was to change from being Messianic "congregations" to becoming Messianic "synagogues." Now, if you have a synagogue, you have to have a rabbi. And then you have to decide what kind of a synagogue you want to be—Orthodox? Conservative? Reform?

Some in the movement created a form of worship such as never existed before—a mixture of Orthodox form and lifestyle with faith in Messiah Jesus—and modeled this form for other congregations. As they did so, more and more Hebrew was incorporated into the service, though few Jews in the United States and almost no Gentiles understood Hebrew. Then the movement decided to call itself "Messianic Judaism" with the not-so-subtle emphasis on the word *Judaism*.

Over the decades more and more rabbinic form and practices were brought into many of the congregations. This emphasis has brought considerable confusion, pain, discomfort and division into the lives of both Jewish and Gentile believers. It also has divided the Church. For these and many other reasons, I agree with David Stern, who wrote, "The American Messianic Jewish movement at present faces a crisis—a crisis of faith."[1]

That is why I am writing this book. I intend to be fair, accurate and comprehensive in my review of Messianic Judaism.

But as you will see, this book also contains an important message for the Church.

1

MESSIANIC JUDAISM

The Issue before Us

I t was about 4:30 on Friday afternoon when the call
came in. I had just finished the sermon I was preparing
for the next Sunday and was ready to quit for the day.
But when I heard the urgency in the voice of my caller,
I knew that something important was taking place.

"Pastor Telchin, my name is Tom. You don't know me,
but I really need to talk with you. Can you spare me a
couple of minutes?"

"Well, yes, Tom," I said. "How can I help you?"

And that opened the floodgate.

For the next fifteen minutes, Tom poured out his
heart to me. He was 21 years old and was not Jewish.
But he wanted me to know that he was in love with
Barbara, a nineteen-year-old Jewish believer in Jesus.
They attended the same Messianic synagogue and had

been dating for more than a year. And she loved him, too. He also loved her parents, and they loved him. And Barbara loved his folks. Their relationship was getting more and more intense, and it looked as if they would get married as soon as he finished school.

"Well, that's good," I said. "So what's the problem?"

The problem, Tom said, was that the rabbi of the Messianic synagogue had invited him to lunch, and when they had finished eating, the rabbi told Tom that his relationship with Barbara was obvious. Then he said that they really needed to break it off.

"Why?" asked Tom.

"Because you're not Jewish," said the rabbi. "Barbara needs to marry a Jewish believer so the Jewish bloodline will be continued."

"What?" I exclaimed. "That's preposterous! Help me understand how all of this happened!"

"Well," said Tom, "I suppose it began when my folks started to attend the Messianic synagogue. You see, my folks love the Jewish people, and they instilled that love in me. A few years ago, when we learned that a Messianic synagogue was opening in our neighborhood, we decided to attend. At first we would go occasionally and go to our church on Sunday. But my folks loved the Jewishness of the synagogue and the wonderful Messianic music and the dancing. They even loved singing songs in Hebrew, though they didn't know what they were singing.

"After about six months, because my folks felt that our church was cold and too formal as contrasted with the synagogue, they decided to leave the church and become members of the synagogue. And I agreed with them. Not much later I noticed Barbara, and I guess she noticed me.

"After a few weeks I asked Barbara out for coffee following the service, and soon we were dating. And before long we were in love.

"No one had told me I should not be dating Barbara. And no one told Barbara that she should not be dating me. We felt that because we were both believers, we would not be unequally yoked. And we were equally committed to living our lives based on the Word of God."

"So far, so good, Tom," I said. "So what happened?"

"Well, a few days ago the rabbi asked me to have lunch with him, and he dropped the bomb on me. Tell me, Pastor Stan, is he right? Should Barbara and I break up?"

I will not share the advice I gave Tom. But as you continue to read, you will grasp and understand the biblical and pastoral response I gave to him.

Questions for Messianic Judaism

I have told you this story to introduce you to a phenomenon that is becoming more and more widespread. With several hundred Messianic congregations in the United States and perhaps an equal number throughout the rest of the world, some serious questions need to be asked and answered in accordance with God's Word:

Are we Jews who have accepted the Messiah "Jewish Christians" or "Messianic Jews"? And is there any difference between the two?

Must we Jewish believers restrict ourselves to attending Messianic synagogues, or may we attend churches?

In what way does my "Jewishness" really matter to God? What about your "Gentileness"?

Are Jewish believers somehow more "special" to the Father than Gentile believers?

Must we call our Messiah "Jesus" or "Yeshua"?

Are "Messianic rabbis" really "rabbis"?

Should Jewish believers who attend Messianic synagogues separate themselves from Jewish believers who attend churches?

Do you really believe that Jewish people can be saved without Jesus?

Is Messianic Judaism a "different gospel"?

What is the role of women in Messianic synagogues?

Should Gentiles be discouraged from becoming members of Messianic synagogues?

Should Gentiles who attend Messianic synagogues cover their heads and wear prayer shawls?

May Gentiles become leaders in Messianic synagogues?

Should Gentile believers convert to some form of Judaism?

May Gentile leaders proclaim themselves to be "Messianic rabbis"?

Should Gentile believers encourage their Jewish friends to attend Messianic synagogues rather than churches?

Should Gentile believers be instructed not to marry Jewish believers?

Do Gentiles have to eat only kosher food and try to obey the Law?

Do Gentile believers in Jesus have to celebrate all of the Jewish holidays?

Do they have to fast on the Day of Atonement?

Should they no longer call themselves "Christians"?

Is Messianic Judaism effective in reaching the Jewish people?

What is the response of traditional Judaism to Messianic Judaism?

Are the teachings and practices of Messianic Judaism consistent with God's Word?

How should Gentile pastors, as well as Gentile believers, respond to Messianic Judaism?

Is the way Messianic synagogues are promoted honest?

Is there such a thing as a separate Messianic Jewish theology?

The list could go on and on.

As you continue to read this book, it will become very clear that, in fact, I do not believe God's Word supports Messianic Judaism. I agree with William Varner, who states, "I do not believe that Messianic Judaism and Messianic synagogues have a biblical, theological, historical or pragmatic justification."[1]

Since I also firmly believe that man learns best from reasons he himself discovers, after you finish reading this book I invite you to come to your own conclusions. Is there a biblical basis for Messianic Judaism? Is it a divisive force in the Body of Christ? How should it be perceived?

My First Experience with Messianic Congregations

I must tell you that when I was first considering the phenomenon of Jews believing in Jesus, I visited a Messianic congregation. The meeting was held in the basement of the leader's home. There I did find Jewish men and women who had confessed Jesus as Lord of their lives. I was intrigued by what I saw because I had been conditioned to believe that no Jews believe in Jesus.

I also was intrigued by the music. It was happy and sounded Jewish. And the congregation seemed to love it. They clapped, and some of them even danced. There was a sense of freedom and joy in these meetings that I had never experienced in my synagogue. The testimony of this congregation showed me that Jews could joyously believe in Jesus.

As I reflect on that period in my life, I recognize that there were some positive aspects to those Friday night meetings. The people were warm and friendly. The sermons were interesting. Support for Israel was evident, and the environment was culturally comfortable.

It is entirely conceivable that I would never have gone into a church to learn more about Jesus. But I did attend this Messianic congregation for several months before I became a believer and for almost two years afterward. That is when I saw some very serious problems surfacing. At that time I remember going to the Lord in prayer: "Father, I don't know what to do. I know that I am not the principal of this school and that I have no right to tell others what or how they should teach. What is it that You want me to do about what I see in Messianic Judaism?"

The response I sensed from Him encouraged me to focus my energies on learning the Word of God and becoming the man He wanted me to be. The Church was His responsibility and not mine. And that settled that.

After I studied to become a pastor, however, I resolved to raise a caution sign to the Church because it seemed to be rushing to embrace Messianic Judaism. I realized the movement needed closer examination. If God's work among the Jewish people was going to flourish, I knew the Church must recognize that the Messianic movement, just like all followers of Jesus, must be held to principles of integrity and commitment to Scripture.

A Disclaimer

At this point I must tell you two very important things. First, I have not attended every Messianic congregation or Messianic synagogue in the United States. Accordingly, the comments that follow do not apply to each and every one of them. I am certain that many are balanced in their theology and practice. My comments are not addressed to them. Second, I again must stress that though I am very closely identified with Jews for Jesus, the opinions in this book are mine and not necessarily theirs. Many of my colleagues attend Messianic congregations and are very happy that they do.

My Beliefs

Over the years I have visited many Messianic synagogues and have attended conferences of Jewish believers in the United States. What I sensed and observed about the theology and practices of these synagogues and conferences have troubled me continually. I believe some of their practices and some of their teachings are unscriptural.

I also have had conversations with many dozens of other Jewish believers in different parts of the world who have expressed their discomfort with the excesses they have observed and experienced in Messianic synagogues. Their points of view have been added to my own and have been incorporated into this text.

Do note that I have used two different words: *congregations* and *synagogues*. In the chapters that follow I will explain the differences between these words. I am not opposed to all Messianic congregations, but I am opposed to Messianic Judaism.

Isn't This an Internal Matter?

Heretofore I have not publicly opposed Messianic Judaism. But now I do. Why? Because I sense that my instructions have changed. Maybe it is because I was involved with the movement for those first two years of my life as a believer and have seen what it did to the Jewish believers I knew then. Maybe it is because for fourteen years I served as pastor of a church made up of both Jewish and Gentile believers. Maybe it is because I have now been to nine nations around the world and observed the divisiveness of Messianic Judaism. For perhaps all these reasons, and especially because of God's prompting my heart, I feel it is now God's will that I stand alongside other Jewish and Gentile leaders who see the dangers of Messianic Judaism and share my concerns with all who have ears to hear.

My Purposes

At this point you could ask: "What is your purpose? What do you hope to accomplish through this book?" Simply stated, I want to accomplish three things. First, it is my hope and prayer that the leaders within Messianic Judaism will accept my challenge to question some of the attitudes and practices of this movement in the light of God's Word. I ask no more of Messianic leaders than I would ask of pastors throughout the Body of Christ. Is what they are doing and teaching really consistent with God's unchanging Word? Or is it possible that they have allowed "Jewishness," "synagogue life," "rabbinic authority," "man pleasing" and "tradition" to do the governing?

It is also my hope that my voice will be perceived as a corrective one to the movement and not a condemning

28

one. I hope I can generate spiritual light rather than the heat of contention. I am not setting out to fight a war. I am a lover, not a fighter. And my overriding objective is to help solve a most serious problem.

My second purpose is to address those who are involved with Messianic Judaism. They need to ask themselves these questions: Are you caught up in the beauty and nostalgia and romance of "Jewishness" to the point

What is your purpose?

that you are ignoring God's clearly stated will that we all are to be "one new man"? (See Ephesians 2:15; we will discuss this concept more thoroughly in chapter 7.) Do you really understand that in His sight there is no difference between Jews and Gentiles?

Finally, because more and more Jewish believers are proclaiming the Messiahship of Jesus every day and receiving Him as Lord of their lives, they—as well as pastors and church leaders everywhere—need to understand the nature of the crisis that is emerging. I am writing this book to help them understand how to respond to Messianic Judaism. I want to help them see why this movement came into being and what they can do to address some of the underlying issues involved.

Second-Class Members?

As you consider the true stories I am about to share, you will gain insight into some of the problems of Messianic Judaism.

Some years ago I was asked to speak at a national meeting of believers in Indianapolis. An entire portion of this meeting was devoted to what God is doing among Jewish people, and I was asked to speak at four of these sessions. Many of the male attendees at these meetings wore head coverings called *yarmulkes* in Yiddish or *kippot* in Hebrew. Some of them wore fringes on their garments. With obvious delight they sat together and joyously sang the Messianic choruses being played. Soon a man got up and began to blast away on a shofar, a ram's horn. Some people laughed and took this as a sign that they were to go to the front and begin to dance. As they did, the rest of the audience began to clap and laugh. They really enjoyed themselves enormously. It was fun to watch.

After the singing and dancing, the messages were shared. I honestly do not remember the content of those messages. And it does not really matter. What matters is that after the meeting, a lovely Gentile woman whom I had come to know approached me and told me how she felt about these meetings.

"They make me feel 'less than,'" she said. "The overwhelming emphasis seems to be on being Jewish and on their belief that Messianic Judaism has it right and the Church has it all wrong." Then she said, "I almost feel as though I am being discriminated against because I am not Jewish!" As a final word she said, "And I've got to tell you, I was absolutely stunned when I heard one of the men say, 'If you don't read the Old Testament in Hebrew, you really cannot understand what is being said.'"

I remember taking her hands in mine as we sat in the empty auditorium and trying to console her. I told her I did not think her reaction was what the speakers wanted her to feel. I suggested that they were just caught up in the wonder and joy of having hundreds of Jewish believers in the same room. I encouraged her to rise above these feelings and know that God loved her and that she was a joint heir with Messiah Jesus. I encouraged her to have patience with these new Jewish believers and not to judge them.

When she felt better, we went our separate ways. Later she wrote me a letter:

Given the deplorable words and acts against Jewish people in which ostensible Christians have engaged over the centuries and the atrocities we have scarcely taken a stand against, I well understand the hostility of Jewish people toward us Christians. But once they accept Jesus as their Messiah, I grieve when there is a continued rift, a remnant of the dividing wall of hostility. I am well aware that, as a Gentile, I am the wild olive shoot grafted into the tree, but sometimes I am made to feel by a very few Jewish brothers and sisters as a second-class member of God's Kingdom, shut out of their society, not part of the real deal.

Before we consider the issues and questions she raised, we have to ask: Is our Gentile friend a little hypersensitive? Do other Gentile believers feel as she does?

But we also must ask: Does the movement harbor an "elitism" that is inconsistent with God's Word? Is pride rearing its ugly head? Why is Jewishness being stressed so much? Is God, after all, a respecter of persons?

Observe the Old Testament Festivals?

Now consider another true story. How would you respond if you—instead of me—had received the following e-mail?

I have a daughter who was born and raised here in a conservative west Michigan Christian home and has accepted Christ as her Savior. She is now living in Southern California and is working with a Messianic Jew. They have been having some wonderful conversations, but

31

now our daughter is really convinced that she must observe the Old Testament festivals in order to be obedient to God. She is trying very hard to convince us that we must do this, too, in order to be obedient to God—and now that we know this, if we do not do it we are being disobedient. This has been very upsetting to us, and she has some very good arguments from Scripture to prove her point.

My question is: How did Christians get so far removed from this? It seems as if nobody pays any attention to the Old Testament festivals. I have asked our pastor about this, and he did not really seem to have an answer for me. I have talked this over with a number of pastors, and all they seem to say is that after Christ came things changed and the focus was on Him, obedience to Him and following in His footsteps. Are there any books that would help me out on this subject? I was in the Christian bookstore yesterday, and they really did not know where to direct me either. I would appreciate any help you could give me.

How would you have answered this e-mail request for help? Do Gentile Christians really need to observe the Old Testament festivals? Do Jewish believers need to do so today? Are they disobedient to God if they do not?

Dilute the Congregation?

Consider a third illustration. Some time ago I was being interviewed by a man we will call Mac who hosted a Christian talk show. After our interview was over, Mac asked, "Stan, would you mind answering a question for me?"

"Certainly not," I replied.

Then Mac told me of an interview he had done some weeks before with a "Messianic rabbi." The interview went well while the rabbi explained how wonderful his congregation was. Then Mac told me that the rabbi addressed the Gentiles in his audience.

"You are welcome to visit us so that you can experience our joy," said the rabbi. "But please don't stay. We don't want to dilute our congregation."

"Tell me, Stan," concluded Mac, "as a Jewish believer, how do you respond to that statement?"

Dear reader, how would you respond?

Gentilized?

Here is a final scene for you to envision. In 1995 I made my fourteenth trip to Israel. While there I ministered in nine congregations. One of them was being led by a Jewish believer from the United States and was referred to as the most "Messianic" of the nine congregations, whatever that means. In attendance at this congregation was a couple I knew when I attended a Messianic congregation after I was saved. The husband was Jewish. The wife was a Gentile. After the service we had coffee together and Lisa (not her real name) turned to me and said, "Stan, would you mind if I asked you a question?"

"Not at all," I said. "What is it?"

"Tell me," she asked, "why aren't you a member of a Messianic congregation? Why are you allowing the Church to 'Gentilize' you?"

At that, I could not help myself and burst into laughter. How was I, a Jew whose parents were both Jewish, going to be "Gentilized" by the Church?

And the circumstances behind the question also amazed me. Here was a Gentile woman married to a Jewish man and living in Israel who seemed to be considering herself "Jewish" and me a "Gentile." She was so very serious that she did not even see the amusing irony in her observation.

I will not tell you what I shared with her, but let me ask you this: As you consider these several illustrations and the questions I have raised, how would you answer them from a biblical perspective?

How would you answer them from a biblical perspective?

Are you beginning to see a tiny part of the problem? Can you see what might happen if the issues involved are not addressed lovingly but firmly?

What We Will Cover

Let me tell you what I would like to accomplish in the rest of this book.

To begin with, I want to review what I believe is the underlying concern—the issue that gave birth to Messianic Judaism. When we understand that, we will better understand how this movement got its start and how it has progressed over the decades. We will also consider whom the movement is reaching. But underlying all of these concerns will be these questions: Is Messianic Judaism biblical? Should the Church encourage Jewish believers to attend Messianic synagogues? How does the movement need to change? How can the Church help?

Let's begin by coming to grips with the issues that gave birth to this movement.

2

WHAT GAVE BIRTH
TO THIS MOVEMENT?

One of the factors that must be fully understood when considering the birth of the Messianic movement is the terrible treatment Jewish people have received at the hands of "Christians" and their churches for most of the past two thousand years.[1] If we do not consider this, then the Messianic movement will make no sense to us.

You will note that I put quotation marks around the word *Christians*. I want to emphasize that using the word *Christian* or "claiming the name of Christ" does not necessarily make one a true disciple of the Lord Jesus. Simply performing acts in His name does not mean that those acts are extensions of His will or Person, or that the people performing those acts truly know Him or are acting within His will.

The Early Church's Treatment of the Jewish People

Before I review the Church's treatment of the Jewish people, I also want to remind you that God's Word is very clear concerning His covenant with and heart attitude toward the people of Israel. In Jeremiah 31 and Romans 9–11 God expresses His never-ending love for us and His future plan for us. If you have not read these portions of Scripture in some time, you might enjoy rereading them before you continue reading this chapter.

Despite God's clear words about the Jewish people, the early Church fathers began to declare that He was finished with us. They began to declare: *Jews killed their Messiah! All of the promises God made to Israel now belong to the Church! God hates the Jews, and we should, too. The only things that await them are the curses of God!*

The early Church fathers repeated this message over the years. Bishop John Chrysostom, the "golden-mouthed," eloquent preacher from Antioch, was one of the most anti-Semitic of all. Chrysostom's eight sermons entitled *Against the Jews* given at Antioch "became the pattern for anti-Jewish tirades making the fullest use (and misuse) of key passages in the gospels of Matthew and John. Thus, a specifically Christian anti-Semitism, presenting the Jews as murderers of Christ, was grafted onto a seething mass of pagan smears and rumors, and Jewish communities were now at risk in every Christian city."[2]

Malcolm Hay adds: "The violence of the language used by St. John Chrysostom in his homilies against the Jews has never been exceeded by any preacher whose sermons have been recorded. . . . [T]hese homilies, moreover, were used for centuries in schools and in seminaries where priests were taught to preach, with St. John Chrysostom as their model—where priests were taught to hate, with St. John Chrysostom as their model."[3]

As strong as the above comments are, they do not give you the flavor or show you the extent of Chrysostom's hatred of the Jews. What I want to restate is that Chrysostom's teaching, as well as that of the other early Church fathers, was repeated year after year, decade after decade and century after century. Indeed, for more than seven hundred years this hatred for the Jews, which the Church advocated, spread until it permeated the Church.

Following is a brief sampling from several of Chrysostom's homilies. (You can find the full text of these eight homilies on the Internet.) In his *First Homily Against The Jews*, he said this:

> Certainly it is the time for me to show that demons dwell in the synagogue, not only in the place itself but also in the souls of the Jews. . . . Do you see that demons dwell in their souls and that these demons are more dangerous than the ones of old?

In his *Fourth Homily Against The Jews*, Chrysostom said this:

> Today the Jews, who are more dangerous than any wolves, are bent on surrounding my sheep; so I must spar with them and fight with them so that no sheep of mine may fall victim to those wolves.

In his *Sixth Homily*, he added:

> You did slay Christ, you did lift violent hands against the Master, you did spill His precious blood. This is why you have no chance for atonement, excuse or defense.

In his *Eighth Homily*, speaking of Christians who go to Jewish doctors, Chrysostom said:

Let me go so far as to say that even if they really do cure you, it is better to die than to run to God's enemies and be cured that way.[4]

Certainly you can understand how these teachings affected those who heard them repeated again and again over the years. All that remained was for bold action to be added to these words—and that is what happened next.

The Crusades

In the year 1095 the Crusades were launched to recover the Holy Land from the Muslims. "The Crusades turned into campaigns of slaughter, rape and pillage, and woe to the poor Jews in the way. Indeed, the Crusades mark the first large-scale mob violence directed against Jews, which is going to become, unfortunately, the pattern for the next hundreds of years. The later pogroms are just going to be a repeat of this idea."[5]

Indeed the Crusaders found many opportunities to put what they had learned from the early Church fathers into practice. Their rage against all nonbelievers certainly included the Jews. And as they struck the Jews in town after town, they were able to repeat their teaching: *The Jews killed Christ. God hates the Jews, and we should hate them, too!*

As the peasant host made its way southward it began to attack and pillage the Jewish communities along the Rhine. About eight hundred Jews were killed in Worms after days of heavy fighting. More than a thousand died in Mainz. They were buried in ditches. In Cologne the synagogue was destroyed. . . . The peasant mob continued southward, offering Jews apostasy or death. Most chose martyrdom.[6]

38

It took you just a moment to read the above paragraph. But think about what you would have felt like if you had been living during that period. Pretend you were a Jewish father who had taken his eleven-year-old son with him one Friday to visit relatives in a nearby town. The next day, Saturday, the Crusaders had entered your town to vent their rage. When they discovered that the Jews were in their synagogue praying, they locked the doors to the synagogue and burned it to the ground. That evening, when you and your son returned home, to your shock you discovered what had been done. The synagogue had been burned to a crisp. Your wife and other children were gone. Your parents, sisters, brothers and neighbors were gone. Only those Jews who had hidden from the Crusaders were alive to tell you what happened. How would you feel at this news? How would you control your grief? Your rage? Your shame? What would you have told your son when he asked, "Why did this happen? What did we do?" Is there any question in your mind about how you would have felt about those "Christians" if you were Jewish?

> *How would you feel at this news? How would you control your grief? Your rage? Your shame?*

The ten Crusades continued in different parts of Europe until 1291. And wherever the Crusaders went, Jews were at risk.

Here is how Abram Leon Sachar reviewed the victories and defeats of the Crusaders:

> It seemed as if the end would never come. Every defeat of the Crusaders brought the wrath of failure; every victory brought the assaults of pride. . . . The Crusades are a turning point in Jewish history. They mark the end of settled Jewish communal life in Europe, the beginning

of intense race-aversions. They usher in the Jewish caricature who stalked through Europe, the pariah with bent
back and hunted look and obsequious manner, bitter
over his yesterdays and fearful of his tomorrows.[7]

There is little doubt that the details of the Crusades
make up one of the ugliest chapters in Church history.
Terrible atrocities, rapes and murders were done in the
name of Christ.

The Inquisition

The impact of the Crusades was experienced in Spain,
too. In America we remember the year 1492 with joy.
That was the year Columbus discovered America. But
what most of us do not know is that on March 31, 1492,
the *Edict of Expulsion* was signed in Granada, Spain. In
this edict, the Jews of Spain were given three choices:
They could convert to Catholicism, leave the country
or be burned at the stake. And they had thirty days to
make their choice. Chaim Potok describes the Spanish
Inquisition:

> On May 1 of that year, Spain began to expel all Jews
> who would not accept Christianity. About 170,000 left
> the land. They went wandering through Europe, Portu-
> gal, North Africa, Turkey. Tens of thousands accepted
> baptism. The last Jew left Spain on July 31, 1492. Spain
> was officially empty of Jews. Pope Innocent III had tri-
> umphed. All the Jews were wanderers, lost in a vast,
> enchanted world.[8]

That is another short paragraph. But again, put yourself into the picture. If you had been living in Madrid
in April 1492, what would you have done? What if your
parents were sick and your wife had just had a baby?

What would you do? Where would you go? Would you leave your parents and flee Spain? How would your wife and newborn baby make the trip? And where could you go? North? You could not go to England. All the Jews of England had been kicked out of England. France? You could not go there either. All the Jews of France had been kicked out of France. South into the Mediterranean? West into the Atlantic? Where could you go to get away from the Church's hate? And how would you feel about these "Christians" who were forcing this crisis upon you?

Despite their fears and their hatred for Christians, many of the Jews of Spain elected to convert to Catholicism. They became known as Marranos. Outwardly they shed their Jewish identity. But in the privacy of their homes, they lived as they had always lived—as Jews. Soon the Church recognized what was happening among these Marranos, and this proclamation was issued: "Any Marrano caught in heresy will be burned at the stake."

What did they mean by "heresy"? If a Marrano wore his best clothes on Saturday, that was heresy. If a Marrano failed to wear his best clothes on Sunday? Heresy! If a Marrano said any Jewish prayers or failed to eat pork, or circumcised his son, or kept any of the Jewish feasts or customs or prepared food according to Jewish law, then he or she was committing heresy! And those convicted of heresy were burned at the stake. Then the Church proclaimed that if an accused Marrano would confess his heresy, the Church would have mercy on him. He would be strangled and burned dead instead of being burned alive.[9]

While we do not have exact figures, it is estimated that almost fifty thousand Marranos were burned at the stake.

The United States lost fifty thousand men and women in the Viet Nam War, and our nation is still suffering.

41

But fifty thousand Marranos were burned at the stake in Spain, and the world knows almost nothing about this—and seems to care even less.

Is there any doubt in your mind about how a Jewish person who knew this history would feel about those "Christians" who murdered his people?

Martin Luther

Martin Luther's challenge of the Church led to the Protestant Reformation. In 1523, after the Church excommunicated him, Luther made the following statement:

> Perhaps I will attract some of the Jews to the Christian faith. For our fools—the popes, bishops, sophists and monks—the coarse blockheads!—have until this time so treated the Jews that if I had been a Jew and had seen such idiots and blockheads ruling and teaching the Christian religion, I would rather have been a sow than a Christian. For they have dealt with the Jews as if they were dogs and not human beings.[10]

Luther made this statement in 1523. But twenty years later, in 1543, because Jews did not rush to become Christians, Luther's message changed drastically and out-Chrysostomed Chrysostom.

Here is what Chrysostom said about the Ark in the synagogue:

> What sort of ark is it that the Jews now have, where we find no propitiatory, no tables of the law, no Holy of Holies, no veil, no high priest, no incense, no holocaust, no sacrifice, none of the other things that made the Ark of the Old Covenant solemn and august? It seems to me that the ark the Jews now have is no better off than

those toy arks, which you can buy in the marketplace. In fact, it is much worse. Those little toy arks cannot hurt anybody who comes close to them. But the ark the Jews now have does great harm each day to those who come near it.[11]

Here is how Luther's anti-Jewish hostility was a reflection of Chrysostom's attack:

First, [Luther] urged, their synagogues should be set on fire, and whatever is left should be buried in dirt so that no one may ever be able to see a stone or cinder of it. Jewish prayer books should be destroyed and rabbis forbidden to preach. Then the Jewish people should be dealt with, their homes smashed and destroyed and their inmates put under one roof or in a stable like gypsies, to teach them they are not masters in our land. Jews should be banned from the roads and markets, their property seized, and then these poisonous envenomed worms should be drafted into forced labor and made to earn their bread by the sweat of their noses.[12]

What a change! Luther's proclamations spread throughout the Protestant world, and from the sixteenth through the eighteenth centuries laws were passed in country after country to segregate and punish Jews. Max I. Dimont expressed the impact of Church denunciations of the Jewish people:

[These laws] not only were aimed at isolating the Jews more and more from the Christians, but [they] were also designed to make them objects of scorn and derision, to deprive them of any symbol of dignity, and to make people forget their former learning. These new laws tended to make Jewish persecutions more and more abstract until the very reason for their origin became obscured, and then forgotten, until only a dehumanized symbol of a denigrated Jew remained. New generations of Christians who did not know of the proud, learned Jew of other days saw only a queerly dressed ghetto Jew wearing a black caftan, a yellow patch of ignominy, a ridiculous peaked hat—an object of derision and scorn.[13]

Again, I ask you, if you were Jewish, how would you feel about the "Christians" who did this to your people?

And How Would You Feel about the Holocaust?

Little needs to be said here about the horrible events of Nazi Germany, World War II and the Holocaust. Many of you may know more about these events than you ever wanted to know. But we must carefully consider and remember how Raul Hilberg summarized the anti-Semitic history, which started with the early Church fathers:

> The missionaries of Christianity had said in effect: *You have no right to live among us as Jews.* The secular rulers who followed had proclaimed: *You have no right to live among us.* The German Nazis at last decreed: *You have no right to live.*[14]

With this history in mind, certainly we can better understand how the Jewish people feel about the "Christians" who persecuted their people. And surely you can understand why Jewish people consider Jews who accept Jesus as Messiah to be "traitors." After my daughter Judy called to tell me that she had accepted Jesus as Lord of her life, I told my wife, "She has just left us and joined our enemies!"

You must understand that the reality of Jesus' Messiahship is not a subject that many Jewish people even consider. Most of my fellow Jews know almost nothing about Him. What we do know, however, and feel is the hatred, discrimination and persecution we have experienced at the hands of "Christians."

There should be little question in your mind as to why many of us do not even want to go into Christian churches. To illustrate this point, consider this true story. A number of years ago, one of my friends who is now a leader in the Messianic movement told me what happened after he first became a believer. "I shared with my wife what had happened to me," he told me. "I wanted her to accept the Lord, too. But she would not budge. Month after month I showed her Scripture and tried to lead her to the Lord. But no luck. Finally she said, 'Okay, I will accept your Jesus, but I will never go into a church!' 'Great,' I told her, 'then I will build you a synagogue.'" Though to my knowledge he never actually built a synagogue for her, I do know that he was very active in helping to organize more than one.

You must understand that the reality of Jesus' Messiahship is not a subject that many Jewish people even consider.

Before I became a believer, I certainly could understand the reasoning behind her statement. In fact, given my background and distrust of Christians, I should have been even less of a candidate for Jesus and Christianity than she was.

In the next chapter I will help you understand why.

45

3

IDENTITY—THE REAL ISSUE

This chapter is largely autobiographical, as I want to help you see a picture of the events that shaped my life. It is important to note that similar experiences shaped the lives of many other Jewish people.

A Jew before Anything Else

If you saw *Fiddler on The Roof,* you may recall the scene when the Russian Cossacks invaded the ghetto in Anatefka. They had one purpose in mind: to vent their hatred and frustrations on all the Jews they met—men, women and children. The scene in the film was very graphic. But the real life experience in Russia as the nineteenth century ended lasted much longer than the film. It went on for decades! Like hundreds of thousands of other Jews, my parents fled Russia to get away from the vicious Cossack attacks.

My father came to America with my grandfather and uncles in 1904. They worked hard for two years to save enough money to bring the women over to New York. By 1907, the family was settled in a tenement apartment building in Manhattan's East Side. Five other Telchin children were born before I came along. I was the youngest and smallest. On September 14, 1924, I made my entrance into the world, weighing two pounds ten ounces. I was a preemie, born in the seventh month of my mother's pregnancy. My folks told me that they kept me in the hospital for seven weeks, fed me with an eyedropper and waited for me to develop so that they could bring me home to our apartment on the fourth floor of the tenement building at 33 Market Street.

When I arrived my mother, Anna, was 44. My father, Hyman, was 48, and my siblings in order were Charlie, 18; Joe, 15; Frances, 14; Sam, 12; and Doris, 2. Mr. Small also lived in our apartment with us. He was a boarder who rented the smallest bedroom and helped pay the rent. Today, I cannot even imagine what it must have been like for nine people to live in five rooms and share one bathroom.

I do not remember very much about those earliest years, but I do know this: I learned that I was a Jew before I was anything else. As I grew up in the ghetto in the late '20s and early '30s, I was reminded continually that I was a Jew. The Gentile kids in our neighborhood called us "kikes" and "greenhorns." But all of the kids living in my building were Jewish.

And soon after I went to public school, I was called a Christ-killer for the first time.

A few years later something else happened that remains vivid in my memory. We were then living in Borough Park, Brooklyn, where I attended PS 131 at Fort Hamilton Parkway and 43rd Street. It was a hot Sunday morning in July 1933, just a few months before my ninth birthday. I was playing stickball in the school yard with my friends. I was a skinny kid and because it was so hot, all I was wearing were shorts and my sneakers. The game was over at noon, and I began to walk down 43rd Street toward our apartment building. As I walked, I looked up and noticed a woman coming toward me. She was wearing a black hat and black dress, and she carried a black book and black purse. As I approached her, her eyes were fixed on me. I was frightened by the expression on her face and just stopped and stood still. She kept walking toward me, closer and closer. Just when I thought she was going to walk right into me, she took a step to the left and with her purse hit me across my chest and said, "Get out of my way, you dirty little kike!" I fell to the ground and began to cry. I thought, *What did I do? Why did she say that?* Then I ran home to my mother. I was crying as I ran up the four flights of steps. When my mother understood what had just taken place, she comforted me and reminded me that I must stay away from the "Christians" because they hated us, and if we got too close to them, sooner or later they would hurt us.

It may be hard for you to imagine a similar scene taking place in your neighborhood, but let me assure you that anti-Semitism was a very real part of American life in those years. Indeed, as I grew older, if anyone asked me my nationality, I knew they were not asking if I was an American—they wanted to find out if I was Jewish! I would stick out my chin and boldly declare, "I am a Jew!"

We avoided people who were not Jewish, and we assumed that everyone who was not Jewish was automatically a "Christian." We had a built-in fear of getting into a disagreement with "Christians," for we believed their hatred for us would rear its ugly head and loose itself upon us. The safest place for us to stay was in the Jewish community, where we would be affirmed and feel safe. And we would stay away from those "Christians."

And yet, along with my brothers and sisters, I wanted to "fit in." We wanted to be regular Americans. We wanted to belong. We did not enjoy being called "greenhorns," the name given to many of the immigrant Jewish families.

Though my parents were from Russia, they rarely spoke Russian. Between themselves and among their children, they spoke Yiddish. We all learned Yiddish, but we wanted to Americanize our parents. We wanted them to learn and to speak English. So when they spoke to us in Yiddish, we would answer in English. In time it worked, and they were able to speak English.

My mother kept a kosher home. She maintained two sets of dishes, pots and pans, silverware, glassware, etc. She kept the utensils she used for dairy dishes away from the utensils she used for nondairy dishes. She never mixed milk with meat. And, of course, we had two other complete sets of dishes, pots and pans, glassware and utensils that were used only at Passover.

Synagogue and Spiritual Life

We only occasionally attended a neighborhood synagogue, since my father worked late on Fridays and all day on Saturday and my mother had her hands full trying to take care of our crowded household. Inevitably, the synagogue played a minor role in our family life. While we observed all the Jewish holidays at home, it was primarily from a gastronomical point of view. My mother would light candles and pray over them before dinner every Friday evening. And for Jewish holidays she would cook all the traditional dishes. When it came time for Rosh Hashanah (the Jewish New Year) and Yom Kippur (the Day of Atonement), things were different. We all looked forward to these holy days and were certain to attend synagogue. Of course, we attended at other times during the year as well, but as I said, overall the synagogue played only a minor role in our Jewish lives.

Over the years as I grew up, I did the things that most good Jewish boys did. I went to Talmud Torah (religious school), where I learned to read Hebrew, but I was never taught to understand what I was reading. At thirteen I became a Bar Mitzvah—a son of the Covenant. Because the year was 1937 and our nation was in the midst of the Great Depression, my Bar Mitzvah celebration took place in our dining room and only four of my friends were able to join the family members who were present. Since then, I have attended many Bar Mitzvah celebrations over the years. You can be sure that I always roll my eyes at the contrast between my Bar Mitzvah and theirs.

Though we were proud of our Jewish heritage, God was not a topic of discussion in our home. The only time I remember my parents talking with me about God was to say, "God forbid" or "God bless you." And the only time I can remember the Messiah being mentioned by my parents was that summer before my ninth birthday in 1933. I asked my parents if I could get a new bike. I will never forget my father's immediate response: "Of course, my son, when the Messiah comes you will get a new bike!"

At age thirteen, soon after my Bar Mitzvah, I joined a Zionist youth group. Here I was taught, and indeed believed, that we Jews had suffered enough. I believed we needed a homeland of our own so that we could live in freedom as Jews. I was very active in this organization throughout my teen years.

Then came World War II. This was a turning point in my life. I sensed that it was now time for me to leave the

Jewish community and defend our nation. On February 16, 1943, at the age of eighteen, I was introduced to my new life at Fort Dix, New Jersey. And for the next 37 months—in different parts of the United States, as well as in France, Luxembourg, Germany and England—I, along with millions of others, set out to rid the world of the Nazi menace and make it safe for democracy.

A Jewish-American

After the war ended, I was admitted to George Washington University in Washington, D.C., where I became extremely active in Hillel, the Jewish center on campus. And during my last two years at GWU, I was a participant in a weekly radio program called *The Jewish Life Hour.*

Later, after college, I took a job with the United Jewish Appeal, which led to a public relations position with the State of Israel Bond Organization, which in turn led to a position with a firm that specialized in fund-raising for Jewish organizations, including B'nai B'rith and Brandeis University. In 1955, after I went into business for myself, 85 percent of my clients were Jewish.

In time we moved into a Golden Ghetto, joined the leading synagogue in town, contributed generously to the United Jewish Appeal, belonged to a Jewish Country Club, gave money to Jewish causes, supported the Hebrew Home for the Aged, and on and on. . . .

With all of that service and sacrificial giving, honors came my way. I became a trustee of this Jewish organization, a board member of another and Man of the Year for still another. It seemed that the more money I gave, the more public honors came my way. I understood this typical social pattern but also was committed to the conviction: "I am a Jew, and we Jews have to take care of our own."

In short, I was immersed in the Jewish community and Jewish life. No matter what else I was, being Jewish was my identity. I was a *"Jewish*-American"!

Jewishness Was Cultural

But what about those Jewish children who came along later—the second, third and fourth generation Jewish kids? How did they define their identity? Were they Jewish-Americans, American Jews or just Americans?

I cannot speak for all who came after me, but I can tell you about my children, my nieces and nephews and the children of my neighbors and friends. I also can tell you about other Jewish adults I have come to know over the decades.

There is no doubt about it: My kids grew up in our good Jewish home. They attended religious school every week during most of their growing up years. My older daughter stayed in religious school until she was confirmed at the age of fifteen. My younger daughter stopped attending right after her Bat Mitzvah.

While we did not even try to keep a kosher kitchen, we did remember all of the Jewish holidays and, once again, celebrated them gastronomically. And, of course, we all attended synagogue on the high holy days and all other key Jewish holidays throughout each year.

But did my kids know anything about God? Not really. Neither did I. And I could not teach them what I did not know. Other than meetings with youth groups at our temple and with B'nai B'rith Girls, they did not regularly participate in other major Jewish religious activities.

Yet they were most certainly Jewish! They were born of Jewish parents. They identified as Jews, and they wanted to be Jews.

My nieces and nephews were not much different from my own kids. They experienced much the same life. They attended religious school and became Bar and Bat Mitzvah. Did they attend their synagogue regularly? No, they did not. But did they identify themselves as Jews and part of the Jewish community? They most certainly did!

Did my kids know anything about God? Not really. Neither did I.

And the other Jewish people I have met over the years? What was their upbringing like? While I have met a few second and third generation observant Jews, the overwhelming majority of the Jewish people I have come to know have not been observant. Like most of the Jewish people in America, including my own family, they have been secular. While they might belong to a synagogue or temple, their infrequent motivation for attending services has been primarily for social, cultural and traditional reasons. While the men might have worn a *tallit* (prayer shawl) and a *yarmulke* (skull cap) when they attended a service, these items did not convey any deep spiritual meaning for them. Their attendance was merely traditional. And in Reform congregations, neither the *tallit* nor the *yarmulke* was required. We did not have to wear anything or do anything. We were just Jews, secure in our awareness of being God's chosen people.

It has been estimated that during the latter half of the twentieth century less than seven percent of the Jewish people in the United States attended synagogue services as often as 24 times a year. For them, apparently, attending synagogue services was no longer essential to their sense of "Jewishness."

Jewish Culture versus Jewish Religion

What should be becoming obvious to you is the difference between Jewish culture and Jewish religion. We were deeply involved in our culture but not in our religion. We were Jews, and we enjoyed Jewish things. We enjoyed Jewish humor, Jewish music and Jewish literature. Those of us who knew Jewish history were proud of our history. Those who were involved in Jewish organizations and/or Jewish causes felt fulfilled by being part of them. In short, we enjoyed being Jewish. And we expressed our Jewishness in a great number of ways. This was easily accomplished. But attendance at synagogue services was widely ignored by most Jews.

To illustrate this point, I placed the word *Jewish* in my search engine. To my surprise, 3,730 sites appeared. Among them were lists of Jewish holidays, Jewish foods, Jewish recipes, Jewish singles, Jewish men's organizations, Jewish women's organizations, Jewish youth organizations, Jewish culture, Jewish music, Jewish charities, the local Jewish community, Jewish family life, Jewish soul mates, Jewish matchmakers, Jewish Holocaust survivors, Jewish delicatessen cookbooks, Jewish fish recipes, kosher recipes, Jewish Marriage Encounters, the World Congress of Gay and Lesbian Jewish Federation, the Jewish Pagan Resource Book, the Jewish Experience, Jewish Children's Bureaus, Jewish War Veterans, Jewish extremism, Jewish philanthropy, basic Jewish jokes, books on Jewish humor—the list went on and on and on.

But Jews and God? Apparently this subject is not important enough to mention. It was not included in the list.

The point I am stressing and frequently repeating is this: Jewish people can express their Jewish identity in innumerable ways; yet, as you will see in the chapters that follow, Messianic Judaism seems to insist that the single most important way a Jewish believer in Jesus can express his or her identity as a Jew is by being part of a Messianic synagogue.

I know of one situation where a Jewish believer who attends a church was described by a Messianic rabbi as no longer wanting to be a Jew. "How is that possible?" he was asked. "Well," said the rabbi, "if he wanted to be a Jew, he would be in a Messianic synagogue. Instead he has become a Christian and goes to a church!"

Can you see the confusion in that statement? Given what you have learned in this chapter about how we Jews express our Jewish "identity," aren't you asking yourself, *How in the world did that Messianic leader come to that conclusion?*

4

How the Movement Grew

Summarizing the growth of the Messianic movement in one chapter is a most difficult—if not an impossible—task. So please consider the information that follows to be a very basic overview.

Jewish Believers Establish Early Congregations

Many Jewish Christians lived in England in the early 1800s. To help encourage and equip them to share their faith with other Jewish people, Congregation *B'nei* (sic) *Abraham* ("Sons of Abraham") was formed in London in 1813. Later, in 1867, the Hebrew Christian Alliance of Great Britain was formed with the same goal in mind.[1]

But in other countries that did not have as many Jewish Christians, no such organizations existed. How, then, were the Jewish people to be reached, motivated and encouraged?

To help you better understand what developed, let's do some role-playing. Go back in time with me to about 1885. Pretend you are a Jewish believer in Jesus living in the city of Kishenev in the Ukraine who felt called by God to share the Gospel with the Jewish people. What would you do? How would you begin?

Perhaps you would look to the Jewish apostle Paul for guidance. In his New Testament epistles, certainly he thought about the Jewish people he was trying to reach. You would do well to follow his instruction and to study the manner in which he tried to evangelize his fellow Jews. You probably would ask yourself some important questions: How observant were they in their Jewish practice? Were they regular synagogue attendees? In what kind of a meeting environment would they be most comfortable? Would it be best to create a separate synagogue for those who had already responded to the Gospel?

As you thought about your people, surely you would know that at that time almost all of them were orthodox in their Jewish practice. (Reform Judaism had not yet been fully established, and Conservative Judaism had not yet gained a strong foothold.) The Orthodox Jews Paul sought to evangelize were very familiar with the liturgy of the synagogue and the Hebrew language. Accordingly, you might come to the conclusion that all Jewish believers would be most comfortable in an environment that looked like a synagogue. That probably was the decision Joseph Rabinowitz made in 1885 when he formed a congregation in Kishenev called Israelites of the New Covenant.[2]

Jewish believers in other parts of the world probably asked themselves similar questions as they reached out to the Jewish people in their communities. In 1930, Congregation Adat Hatikvah was organized in Chicago,

Illinois. And the First Hebrew Christian Church was formed in Buenos Aires, Argentina, in 1936.[3]

Not Only Jewish Believers

But Jewish believers were not the only ones who wanted to reach the Jewish people. As early as 1833, a Gentile Dane named John Nicolayson arrived in Jerusalem, where for the next 23 years he sought to share the Gospel with Jewish people in Palestine. While there, he also established a congregation for all who responded. It was named Christ Church and was widely known as "the oldest Protestant Church in the Mideast."[4]

And in America there were also many missionaries to the Jewish people. Working with Jewish believers, they helped form the Hebrew Christian Alliance. Most of the Jewish members of the Alliance were immigrants to the United States from Europe. They were largely biblical in their beliefs, very conscious of their "Jewishness," active in opposition to anti-Semitism and supportive of the Zionist movement with its call for reestablishing the State of Israel. They also continued to share the Good News of Messiah Jesus with other Jewish people.[5]

A Change in the Name of the Alliance

In the United States, an effort was launched in 1973 to change the name of the Hebrew Christian Alliance to the "Messianic Jewish Alliance." The motivation behind this was to avoid using the word *Christian*, which offended many Jewish people who felt threatened by the implied connection with anti-Semitism. This provoked many debates with the older British Hebrew Christian Alliance, whose early leaders were mostly dead by the middle of the twentieth century and, thus, not around to defend the name. Even though many of the old guard in the United States objected to this name change, by 1975 the change was formally adopted.[6]

Alliance Leaders Who Encouraged Changes

Martin Chernoff became president of the Hebrew Christian Alliance of America in 1971, just before the name change, and spearheaded a stronger move toward rabbinic tradition. He served until 1975 and was later followed by his two sons, Joel (who served from 1979 to 1983) and David (1983–1987). During these years a new terminology was created. In addition to the change in the name of the Alliance, Jews were no longer "converted"; they were "completed." The church was "the congregation" or even "the synagogue," biblical names were to be pronounced in their supposed original Hebrew form and so on.[7]

Joe Finkelstein and his wife, Debbie, were also active in changing the nature of the Alliance. Unlike the majority of Messianic leaders, Joe came from a Conservative Jewish background and Debbie was Orthodox. They attracted many Jewish and Gentile young people, some of whom professed conversion and joined together in worshiping at the Finkelsteins' home. Joe repeatedly insisted that there is no contradiction between being Jewish and believing in Jesus. He and his wife maintained a traditional Jewish lifestyle, which soon was adopted by many of their young adherents.[8]

Practical Results of Changing the Alliance

What were the practical results of the decision to change the name and nature of the Alliance? To begin with, if you have a "synagogue," then you have to have a "rabbi." In 1975, I was part of Beth Messiah Congregation in Rockville, Maryland, led by Manny Brotman, another of the strong Alliance leaders. I remember when Manny announced at one Friday night service that he was henceforth to be known as Rabbi Brotman. I was shocked at his announcement. A few days later, I called Manny and asked him to have lunch with me. At lunch I explained to Manny the rigorous *yeshiva* (seminary) training and the *smicha* (ordination) that is required before one can be proclaimed a "rabbi" in traditional Judaism. I explained that a congregation or a movement not constituted for that purpose cannot bestow the title. And, I stressed, an individual most certainly cannot bestow the title upon himself.

I then told Manny that his self-proclamation as a rabbi was insensitive and would be an offense to the very Jewish people he wanted to reach. Manny countered by telling me that Messianic Judaism was becoming a reality and that it would become the fourth branch of Judaism, along with Orthodox, Conservative and Reform Judaism. I was stunned by Manny's statement and asked, "Don't you understand Judaism? Though the different branches disagree among themselves on many things, the one issue that unites them is their conviction that Jesus is not the Messiah."

Manny thought for a moment and then said, "We're going to change that!"

At this point there was little I could add, and the discussion ended.

As more and more leaders in the movement caught the idea, many of them began to call their congregations "synagogues" and proclaimed themselves to be "rabbis." But most of these men were not raised as observant Jews, most had no rabbinic training and some of them were Gentiles. I remember thinking, *How can they* ever *expect to be considered rabbis by the Jewish community? Won't there be strong opposition to their use of this term?*

As time went on, and probably as an effort to avoid opposition from the Jewish community, they began to call themselves "Messianic rabbis." Who would challenge that title?

Messianic Leaders Out of Touch

At the beginning of this chapter, I pointed out that in the 1880s and early 1900s most of the Jewish people were orthodox in their religious practice. But by the 1970s the overwhelming majority of Jews in America was secular and did not attend synagogue. I also listed some of the many things that make up Jewish life and Jewish interests. But the significance of these facts seemed to elude the leaders of Messianic Judaism. They were determined to establish Messianic synagogues and promote the movement. They also were more focused on maintaining Jewishness than they were on maintaining the integrity of Scripture. As we move into the next chapter, I will take a look at why these leaders were so determined.

5

IS MESSIANIC JUDAISM
JEWISH?

Messianic Judaism declares that one of its primary objectives is to reach other Jewish people with the Gospel. I applaud that objective and certainly share it. God's Word tells us that He does not want any to perish but all to receive eternal life. And this includes the Jewish people.

Another stated objective is to provide fellowship for Jewish believers. This, too, is a very important objective.

But pay careful attention to the next statement: Gaining acceptance by the Jewish community seems to have become one of its primary objectives. Hear me clearly as I rewrite that statement: As Jews who believe in Jesus, Messianic Jews want to be identified with and accepted by a Jewry that has largely rejected God and His Word. Clearly this is not a biblical objective.

Maintaining "Jewishness" versus Maintaining Scripture

The last chapter ended with the statement that Jewishness, rather than Scripture, seems to be a very strong emphasis of Messianic Judaism. If we remove the Bible from our consideration, we are left only with the opinions of men. And the strong and emotional arguments of some of the more charismatic leaders in the movement can be very persuasive.

As you read the statements that follow, be sure to remember that you are reading the opinions of men and not the Word of God. Remember, too, that it is God's Word and not the opinions of men that should govern our lives.

And as you examine the statements made by leaders in the Messianic movement, please be aware that there are a great number of differences in biblical understanding, liturgy and practice among the different Messianic congregations. And there are extremes at each end. So please do not think that these statements apply to all Messianic congregations.

To help you better understand the nature of these differences, you might want to go to your search engine and type in the words *Messianic Judaism*. Do not be surprised if more than 33,000 sites appear. You would probably never take the time to visit each of these sites, but if you visit even a few dozen of them, you will find a variety of descriptions of and explanations for Messianic Judaism. And you surely will see that most of them are focused more upon "Jewishness" than upon the Bible.

> *If we remove the Bible from our consideration, we are left only with the opinions of men.*

Jews Must Not Be Gentilized

Messianic leaders argue, for example, "We Jews must not be Gentilized in Christian churches but must be allowed to express our faith in Yeshua (the Hebrew name of Jesus) in Jewish ways." And so many times I have heard them say, "Koreans have Korean churches. Hispanics have Hispanic churches. Why can't we Jews have Messianic synagogues?" That argument does not hold up in the face of reason. Yes, first-generation Korean believers who come to the United States and who do not speak English hold their services in Korean. But second- and third-generation English-speaking Korean-Americans can be found in many churches around our nation. They do not *have* to belong to Korean-speaking churches. And they are not criticized as "not wanting to be Korean anymore" if they do not attend Korean churches.

The argument also falls apart when you look at Jewish people today. Most of us do not speak Hebrew. Most are not regular synagogue attendees. Most do not equate being Jewish with participating in synagogue life. So why should we be *required* to attend a Messianic synagogue when we come to faith *in order to prove that we are Jewish?*

The Jewish Jesus Has Been Gentilized

These leaders also say, "There is much 'alien' culture that surrounds Gentile Christianity, which makes it unpalatable to most Jewish people. Jews will nearly always reject the Gentile Jesus as being the Messiah but will much more readily accept the Jewish Yeshua as being their Messiah."[1]

Is that statement accurate? Consider: As will be more fully treated in a later chapter, almost all Jewish believers will testify that they were not saved in—nor do they attend—Messianic congregations or synagogues. In almost all cases, they were saved because caring Gentiles shared the Gospel with them. And they attend churches. This also certainly helps explain the results of a "Jewish Believers Survey" for the period 1986–1991, which showed that "only four percent of believing Jews were evangelized by Messianic congregations."

What Are We to Be Called?

"Most Messianic Jews refrain from calling themselves 'Christians,' which is Greek terminology. They prefer more Hebraic terms, such as 'Messianic Jews.'"[2]

Is that statement accurate? Consider: Before the late 1970s the words *Messianic Jews* were hardly ever heard. Today the movement appears to want to make a major distinction between "Messianic Jews" and "Jewish Christians." "Messianic Jews," they allege, attend Messianic synagogues, while "Jewish Christians" attend churches. Despite this sharp distinction the movement seeks to make, I suspect that the majority of Jewish believers today call themselves "Messianic Jews," even though they are not involved with Messianic Judaism. They refuse the term *Judaism* because it reminds them of rabbinic—man-made—concepts, which they refuse as contrary to Scripture.

After the destruction of the Temple in Jerusalem in 70 AD, the Jewish leadership was in a quandary. How were they to obey God's ordinances without the sacrifice system in the Temple? How were they to live as Jews without the Temple? Soon a number of rabbis went to the town of Yavneh and began to work on developing

Jewish practices and liturgy. These practices and the liturgy that emerged were "man-made"—made by the rabbis—and often were not biblical.

Jewish believers today recognize that rabbinic Judaism is a religion alien to the New Covenant faith. Michael L. Brown points out that rabbinic Judaism does not even claim to be based upon a literal interpretation of the Scriptures. Instead the rabbis say that their faith is the continuation of an unbroken chain of tradition dating back to Moses.[3] Many others would say, "We have gotten our eyes off of Yeshua and onto religious forms. And for many, the problem has been an overemphasis on the mind and academic study coupled with an underemphasis on prayer and life in the Spirit. Rabbinic Judaism, with its stress on study and intellectual prowess, and with the soulish beauty of many of its customs, has lured some believers away from the simplicity of their faith in Yeshua."[4]

Zealous for the Law

Then they say, "Most Messianic Jews are much more 'zealous for the Law (Torah)' than their Gentile Christian counterparts. In this, they are following the example of the first century Messianic Jews, who were also 'zealous for Torah' (see Acts 15:19–21; 21:17–26)."[5]

Are these statements accurate? Consider: The Torah contains 613 commandments from God that are binding upon the Jewish people. Do those who attend Messianic synagogues even know these 613 commandments? And if they do not know them, how can they zealously keep them? What they seem to be zealous for is the word *Torah* and the emotional coloring of carrying the Torah scrolls around the synagogue during a service. Also, the first-century Jewish believers were living the life they had always lived and following the practices that were normal for them. They did not have to learn an entirely new liturgy and then live their lives by it.

Forcing Gentile Culture upon Jews

"It is wrong and unscriptural to force Gentile Church culture upon the Jewish people as a requirement for believing in their own Messiah. While it is right and proper for other cultures to be allowed to practice their culture after coming to faith in Yeshua, much of Jewish culture comes directly from the Scriptures and has a firm biblical foundation lacking in other cultures."[6]

> *Those in Messianic Judaism seem to have created a liturgy that never existed before and are forcing it upon Gentiles, as well as those Jews who attend their congregations.*

Is the focus of that statement correct? Consider: Quite the reverse is true. No one is "forcing" Gentile Church culture on Jewish believers as a requirement for belief in Messiah Jesus. But as I said above, those in Messianic Judaism seem to have created a liturgy that never existed before and are forcing it upon Gentiles, as well as those Jews who attend their congregations. They declare that what they are practicing is "biblical Judaism." Nothing could be further from the truth. Biblical Judaism requires a system of sacrifice. "For the life of a creature is in the blood, and I have given it to you to make atonement for yourselves on the altar" (Leviticus 17:11).

What my brothers in the movement mean, perhaps, is that they are following rabbinic Judaism by "celebrating" the feasts of Israel. The Jewish roots of our faith

68

deserve recognition, and there is absolutely nothing wrong with remembering God's faithfulness to His covenant people as we celebrate the feasts. But it is God and not the feasts that are to be worshipped. And it is wrong to require that Gentiles must observe these feasts in order to please God.

Keeping Kosher

"Messianic Jews tend to observe biblical kashrut (laws of clean and unclean meats)" (see Leviticus 11; Deuteronomy 14).[7]

Is that statement accurate? Do they really keep "kosher"? Perhaps a few might, but the overwhelming majority does not. Indeed in most of American life today, it is extremely difficult, if not impossible, to keep a truly kosher kitchen without having a major alteration in lifestyle and at great expense. And "keeping kosher" does not just cover what happens in your home. It means that no matter where you go you *never* eat foods that are not kosher and are not prepared in accordance with the rules of *kashrut*—the rabbinic expansion and detailed legalizing of the procedure for preparing kosher foods.

Pause now for just a moment in order to focus on the flip side of this argument: Gentiles trying to keep kosher. "Sharon," a young Jewish woman I know, told me of an event that happened when she was a member of a Messianic synagogue. She said: "One strange experience I had occurred one morning when I, along with several other women of the congregation, were traveling home from a women's retreat. We stopped at a restaurant to eat breakfast, and when it came time to order, every one of the women requested that no meat be served with her eggs. This was because they did not want to eat pork. I happened to be the only Jew in the group, and

I really wanted to have some bacon, but when it came my turn to order, I requested no meat as well so as not to make any of my Gentile companions stumble" (see 1 Corinthians 8:13).

The Appeal to Gentiles

"Most Messianic assemblies have a large percentage of Gentiles. These Gentiles love Israel and the Jewish people and have adopted a Jewish expression of their faith in Messiah Yeshua."[8]

As reported by almost all who have experienced these congregations, the overwhelming majority—sometimes as much as 85 to 90 percent of the attendees—are Gentiles. Certainly they are being blessed. But the movement's primary declared objective was not to bless Gentiles. It was to reach Jews. Are they doing that? Are they appealing to Jewish people? Are they sharing the Gospel? We will consider these questions a bit later.

The Reaction of the Jewish Community

All of the statements by the Messianic community that I have just mentioned are indicative of how the movement seeks identification with and acceptance by the Jewish community—a community that, as I said earlier, has largely rejected God and His Word, and certainly has rejected Messiah Jesus. This is an objective that is highly unreachable.

I agree with Arnold Fruchtenbaum who says, "It is self-deceiving to believe that a Jewish lifestyle is the means of being accepted by the Jewish community or the Jewish leadership."[9] The traditional Jewish community abhors Messianic Judaism. We Jews may be divided on all sorts of issues, but the one thing we agree upon is that belief in Jesus is a threat to our Jewishness. We have somehow come to equate the word *Christian* with the word *Gentile*. Accordingly, many believe that if a Jewish person accepts Jesus, he becomes a "Gentile" and can no longer be a Jew. If this is true, how can those who support the movement declare that it is accomplishing one of its primary goals: to "bring the Gospel to the Jewish people"?

For these reasons, you must understand that the Jewish community will do all in its power to prevent the favorable recognition of Messianic Judaism. Some time ago, I heard a rabbi say that there are no Jews who believe in Jesus!

"How can you say that?" I asked.

"Very simple," he replied. "The moment they believe in Jesus, they cease being Jews!"

What an unbiblical statement.

To further emphasize this point, look at the State of Israel, which also seems to be confused by the question of who is a Jew. Many in Israel seek to deny the *Right of Return*—whereby any Jew may become a citizen of Israel—to Jews who believe in Jesus.

What Does "Being Jewish" Mean?

In order to be a Jew, a person must be born of Jewish parents. It does not matter what his or her parents believe or what the person himself or herself believes. Many of us are quite comfortable with Jewish Hindus, Jewish Buddhists, atheistic Jews, agnostic Jews, Orthodox, Conservative or Reform Jews. We even can understand humanistic Judaism. The Jewish community does not have any trouble continuing to call these people Jews.

But when a Jewish person accepts Jesus, the situation changes. Why? Because so many Jewish people have bought into the rabbis' repeated slogan: "You cannot be Jewish and believe in Jesus." When it comes to followers of Jesus, by whatever name they choose to identify themselves, the line in the sand is drawn. These people are not welcome. What that has to tell you is that those in Messianic Judaism fool only themselves when they insist that they soon will receive approval from the Jewish community.

To emphasize this point, consider this important quote: "Messianic Judaism is very far from finding acceptance among their fellow Jews who do not believe in Jesus. This truth should give rise to serious thought about the viability and justification of the movement."[10]

In addition to being born of Jewish parents, being "Jewish" includes sharing Jewish history, culture and concerns and identifying one's self as a Jew. It means understanding Jewish humor and Jewish grief. Some would say that it also means enjoying Jewish foods. If indeed these are valid indicators of "Jewishness," are they found in Messianic congregations? Despite their love for the Jewish people, since most of the members of these congregations are not Jewish, they cannot share Jewish identity. And again you must see that wearing a *kippah* (skull cap) and a *tallit* (prayer shawl), putting on *tvillin* (phylacteries), lighting Sabbath candles, singing Hebrew songs and dancing to Messianic music do not transform a Gentile into a Jew. And certainly, not wearing or doing these things does not take a Jewish person's identity away from him or her.

But by focusing on rabbinic form and synagogue life, Messianic Judaism hopes to gain acceptance by the Jewish community. It also seeks to help its adherents displace the fear that has been programmed into them by rabbinic teaching. That fear screams, "By accepting

Jesus you have betrayed the Jewish people, and you are no longer Jewish." By stressing attendance at a Messianic synagogue, they hope to be able to say, "We are so Jewish! We are more Jewish than ever before. Look what we do in our synagogue."

Earlier I pointed out that Baruch Maoz wrote a book titled *Judaism Is Not Jewish*. Based upon the above and despite the emotional and intellectual protestations we can expect from the movement, would you expect he would probably also say that Messianic Judaism is not Jewish?

Once again, I emphasize that there are the Jewish people and Jewish culture. Then there is the Jewish religion. They are not the same. Although Jews show great indifference to a Jewish person's religious beliefs, they rule out any thought of the retention of his Jewishness if he confesses faith in Jesus as his Messiah.

> But the truth of the matter is that believing in Jesus, the Jewish Messiah, is one of the most Jewish things a Jewish person can do.

But the truth of the matter is that believing in Jesus, the Jewish Messiah, is one of the most Jewish things a Jewish person can do.

6

THE PHENOMENON

Gentiles in Synagogues

What is it about Messianic congregations that attracts so many evangelical Gentiles? Over the years I have asked this question of a great many Gentiles in the movement. Some have said, "The church I attended was cold and unresponsive. It is not that way here. I love the music and the dancing. I actually feel Jewish when I come here." Others have answered, "It puts me in touch with my Jewish roots." Still others have said, "I love the Jewish people and want to share my love with them," or, "I believe that God has a special plan for the Jewish people in these last days, and I want to be part of it."

The issue—indeed, the phenomenon—of Gentiles attending Messianic synagogues is a critical one when considering the validity of the Messianic movement.

As we begin to explore this, let us first consider some specific responses I received from Gentiles in different parts of the United States when I asked them what attracted them to the movement.

Laura

I met "Laura" when I spoke at a very moderate Messianic synagogue—one that utilizes only those elements of traditional services that are completely free from the rabbis' omissions or changes and are more biblical. I called Laura and told her I was doing a new book and that in one of the chapters I wanted input from Gentiles about why they attend Messianic synagogues. "Would you please help me understand why you do?" I asked.

I wrote down her response: "Initially the catalyst for me was the woman who led me to the Lord. She had a heart for Jewish evangelism and instilled it in me. Years later, when I attended a Messianic synagogue for the first time, I felt that I was home. The worship and sense of community are so real and precious that they keep me there. I do not attend any other church. I also want to share what I have experienced with others and to help them become part of it. I want them to know that the Gospel is for the Jew first."

At this point, Laura seemed to stop to gather her thoughts. Then she made these two points: "The primary reason I go is that I feel the Lord has called me there. I see the prophetic way God has designed it—that we be together and that we be one. Second, I need to tell you about a Torah service that took place one day at our community Bible study. It was here that a real healing took place. The meeting was held in a church, and it was awesome when our guest teacher, a Jewish man, got up to read in Hebrew from the Torah. There was a healing from all of the years of distrust, torment and pain caused by the anti-Semitism of the past."

Again she paused to think and added, "If you want to sum up my position, you could say that though I am not Jewish, I am a Ruth."

Then Laura made this interesting observation: "But I also need to add this thought: There is something that concerns me. It is the emphasis on the 'doing' rather than on the 'being.' I sometimes hear more about the movement than I do about Yeshua. This is one of the biggest errors I see. We have been called to 'be' His disciples. We must 'be' before we 'do.'"

Sheila

"Laura" introduced me to "Sheila" at a community Bible study group I addressed. Sheila wrote to me after the meeting, so I had her address and phone number. I called Sheila and we talked on the phone for a bit. When I asked her why she attended a Messianic synagogue, she said, "When I attended the synagogue it was like Galatians 3:28 coming alive before my very eyes: 'There is neither Jew nor Greek, slave nor free, male nor female, for you are all one in Christ Jesus.'"

Later Sheila sent me an e-mail in which she wanted to more fully explain her feelings. Here are some of the things she wrote:

> I was familiar with the passages in Romans 11 about how the Gentile has been grafted into the tree, and I was grateful to God that He had grafted me in; however, I never pursued the passage any further. I did not understand then, as I do today, that God was saving the Gentiles through the "partial hardening" of His beloved Israel, that we in turn through our salvation might provoke the Jewish people to jealousy (see Romans 11:11).

It was at this point that you came to our Bible study and gave your testimony of salvation, and my heart leaped. Then, when I heard that you would be speaking at a Messianic synagogue in town, I knew that I had to hear your message. You spoke about the Church's anti-Semitism over the centuries, which has been a major factor in keeping Jewish people from the Gospel. I wanted my husband to hear you. I wanted my church to hear you. I want and hope for every believing Gentile I know to hear your message—God's message—of hope "first for the Jew, then for the Gentile" (Romans 1:16).

I know we also spoke about the Torah service that was hosted at the end of study this year. Again it was one of the most beautiful and moving services I ever attended. In just this one service, I saw aspects of God that I had never seen before. I shared with you how for the first time in my Christian life I saw the Bride of Christ in the service. The service began with a woman who prayed for God's blessing, mercy and protection over the morning worship. It was an anointed prayer and one given by a woman. It is not customary in my denomination for a woman to lead the congregation in prayer during a formal worship service, and I was not accustomed to seeing women participate in a service. My eyes and ears were opened. I looked for what God might want to show me through this woman. After the opening prayer, a married couple performed the blessing of the wine and the bread. Before he drank from the cup the husband gave the cup to his bride, and she drank first. I was so struck by the husband freely and lovingly giving his wife the first sip. It was such a picture to me of Christ freely and lovingly giving Himself and His blood for His Bride.

Later the women led us in performing what they called Davidic dancing. I was so touched by the humility and modesty of their dance and the way in which each dancer seemed to be fixing her eyes and heart on the Lord. It was both reverent and humble, yet what impressed me even more was how intimate and confident each woman seemed to be before her Lord. They were not dancing for each other or for the praises of men, but for Christ. And we in the congregation were blessed by their genuine expression of love for Him. I also was struck by the loving gaze each of the men cast toward the dancers. Again, I saw a picture of my Lord gazing upon His beloved Bride as she danced with joy and love for her Savior, her Bridegroom. There is so much more, but these were my lasting impressions.

It is entirely possible that the above statements represent the views of many Gentiles who attend Messianic synagogues.

Fred and Glenda

I also called "Fred" and "Glenda," a lovely, older Gentile couple. I asked them why they attended their Messianic congregation. Fred told me they had been going for about eight years—indeed, ever since their congregation started. Though they are Gentiles, Fred said, "We have a supernatural relationship with the Jewish people." Then he went on, "We feel that the Lord showed us in 1980 that He has something special in His heart for Israel. We decided that we had to learn more about the Jewish people and the feasts of Israel. We wanted to know about Passover, Pentecost, Rosh Hashanah, Yom Kippur and Tabernacles. So we started to attend an Orthodox and then a Conservative synagogue and asked lots and lots of questions in the informal discussions that followed. We were hungry to learn. And the more we learned, the more we realized that some of the things the Church celebrates today are really human creations and biblically inappropriate."

"Like what?" I asked.

"Well, like Easter. This started out as the Feast of Eshtar, a pagan holiday. Why the Church adopted the words *Easter Sunday* instead of *Resurrection Sunday* I do not think I will ever understand."

Then Glenda spoke up: "We also enjoy seeing the two branches of the Church come together—the Jewish branch and the Gentile branch. Why should we not worship the Lord together? Knowing what we know now is so much deeper than what we knew before. And I love the dancing in our congregation. I am part of the dance troupe."

"How big is your congregation, and do you meet on Friday nights as well as on Saturday mornings?" I asked.

Glenda responded, "We have between twenty and fifty on any given Saturday morning. This is the only weekly meeting we have."

"How many are Jewish?" I asked.

"Oh, I guess about one-third," Fred replied.

"Do you also attend a church?" I asked.

"Oh yes, we do," Fred replied. "And we love our church, too."

Charlie and Fran

I also posed the question to "Charlie," a Gentile in his late fifties. When I asked Charlie what drew him to a Messianic synagogue, he said, "I began to attend a Messianic synagogue shortly after I married 'Fran,' my Jewish wife, who was not yet a believer. I really wanted Fran to receive the Lord, but initially she was quite resistant. I felt that if I brought her to a Messianic synagogue, it might be easier for her to receive Yeshua."

"So what happened?" I asked.

"Well," Charlie said, "she did receive the Lord. I'll let her tell you how that happened."

"I attended the synagogue with some trepidation," Fran said. "But I was moved by the music. As a matter of fact, it was the wonderful Messianic music that got me. Growing up in Texas in a Reform congregation, I had never heard it before. I had been searching for a bridge between Christianity and Judaism, and for me music was the bridge that closed the greatest, most tragic schism in all human history. I loved it and still love it."

"I know what you mean," I said. "I love Messianic music, too. There is nothing like it. It is filled with joy. And do you want to hear something funny?" I asked. "I once heard a Gentile minister of music say that you cannot worship the Lord in a minor key. Boy, was he ever wrong!" I laughed.

Then I addressed Charlie. "Tell me, Charlie, did you stay in the synagogue very long?"

"Well, we stayed for about a year and a half," he replied. "But then I began to be troubled by what I observed, and Fran was equally troubled."

"By what?" I asked.

"Well, from a theological point of view, it seemed as if they were concentrating on emulating rabbinic Judaism with a Christian vocabulary rather than concentrating on the finished work Jesus did on the cross. This thereby encouraged Gentiles to do things that Gentiles were never required to do in Scripture. We Gentiles never had to wear *yarmulkes* (head coverings) or *tallits* (prayer shawls) or *tsitsit* (fringes on our garments). Yet the implication was that if we wanted to belong, we had to wear them. And there were so many Gentiles in attendance! More than eighty percent of those who came each week were not Jewish. Why did they have to do these things? As a matter of fact, I began to wonder about the purpose of the congregation. They said they wanted to reach Jewish people by making the place more comfortable for them, but that was not what was happening.

"They also seemed to be clouding the issue for Jewish people. As believers, did they still have to do A, B, C and D, or was God's grace sufficient for them after they received the Lord?"

Then Fran jumped into the conversation. "The Gentiles who attended seemed to be worshipping the symbols of Judaism. Isn't that idolatry?" she asked. "And I know of a Gentile couple who went to an Orthodox rabbi and converted to Judaism. The husband was circumcised, and they tried to keep a kosher home. And for others, there seemed to be an identity crisis. Some of the Gentiles I met began to search their family tree in order to find a Jewish relative. They wanted to be Jewish, and they tried to live by the Law. They did not seem to understand Romans 13:8, which tells us that love fulfills the Law."

> "As believers, did they still have to do A, B, C and D, or was God's grace sufficient for them after they received the Lord?"

Then Fran added, "If you want to know what really did it for me and why I insisted that we leave that congregation, I'll tell you. I was filled to overflowing by the 'wannabes' and the 'Pharisees'!"

I did not think I needed to ask any more questions to know how Fran felt.

Why Gentiles Attend Messianic Synagogues

The reasons that these Gentile believers give for attending Messianic synagogues are typical of the reasons described to me over the past 25 years by Gentile believers around the country. Based upon responses such as these, I can understand why Gentiles are attracted to Messianic congregations. They love the music. They want to learn about the Jewish roots of their faith. They enjoy learning about the Jewish holidays and even enjoy singing Hebrew songs. And certainly they enjoy the feeling of being a family.

And yet the problems they mention also are found across the board and highlight my purposes for writing this book.

Why Jews Do Not Attend Messianic Synagogues

So why don't Jews attend?

It is very difficult to say how many Jewish believers there are or where they go to worship the Lord, because to the best of my knowledge no such records are available. Some say the United States alone has more than a hundred thousand Jewish believers in Jesus. I cannot verify that. But I can tell you that based upon the dozens and dozens of people with whom I have discussed this question, I know that the overwhelming majority of Jewish believers do not attend Messianic synagogues. It has been suggested to me that less than five percent of the Jewish believers in the United States attend them.

Why is that? Perhaps it is because those who had an Orthodox or Conservative upbringing in the synagogue are uncomfortable with what they see and hear in most Messianic synagogues. It is something they never saw or heard in their home synagogues. Many Jewish people who I have brought to such synagogues have told me they felt as though they were looking at a caricature—an imitation and not the real thing.

But perhaps the major reason why more Jewish followers of the Messiah are not involved in Messianic
Judaism is that most Jewish people in the United States
did not grow up in observant homes or in the synagogue. They find the Messianic synagogues foreign to
their understanding and choose to stay away. "Fran,"
you will recall, pointed out that she was raised in a
Reform congregation in Texas and that the liturgy of
the Messianic synagogue was totally foreign to her. As
she said, and based upon what I have observed over the
years in many Messianic congregations, God's love and
grace are secondary to the emphasis upon "Jewishness."
This, too, drives many Jewish believers away.

Jean

"Jean" is a young Jewish mother of two beautiful children. She attended a church before she met her future
Jewish husband, but when they decided to marry, he
convinced her to attend his Messianic synagogue. She
agreed to do so, and for several years they rarely missed
a service. Then things began to change. When I asked
Jean what it was that disturbed them, she said, "I want
to be very careful about how I answer that question, so
let me put my thoughts in writing to you."
A few weeks later, Jean wrote to me:

I have been agonizing as I have relived the experiences
we had at the Messianic synagogue and why we left.
Simply stated, I was at once saddened and angry by the
way so many of my Gentile brothers and sisters—who
made up about 85 percent of the congregation—showed
almost a contempt toward God by despising what He
had made them to be. I felt they did this when they
dressed as Jews and adopted all sorts of religious tradi-

tions that they convinced themselves they were obligated to practice.

Week after week I would anguish over the emphasis on Jewishness rather than "Jesusness." Gentiles were changing their names to Jewish-sounding ones and calling themselves Jews. And then there was this: Anti-Semitism within the Church was occasionally highlighted in the sermons and teachings, but the great things done by many of the Church fathers were never mentioned. A sort of reverse anti-Semitism existed in the form of anti-Church sentiment. You were made to feel you would be betraying those in the synagogue if you were to leave the Messianic congregation to attend a church. You would be perceived as one who was "siding with the enemy" of the Jewish people. My husband and I agreed about our concerns and went to the rabbi with them. But even though it was agreed that our issues were legitimate, nothing ever changed. Because of the many friends we had in the congregation it took some doing, but because we understood what was happening in the synagogue, we knew we had to leave. And we did.

Not All Congregations Are Like That

As I was writing this chapter, I called a friend of mine who leads a Messianic congregation and discussed this phenomenon with him.

"I understand," he said. "What many in the movement are doing is substituting rabbinic form for Jewish culture. We don't do that in my congregation. The only things I do on Saturday mornings are blow the *shofar* [ram's horn] to announce the beginning of the service. And we sing the *Sh'ma* (the watchword of our faith from Deuteronomy 6:4 that begins, 'Hear, O Israel: the LORD our God, the LORD is One'). We do not wear *yarmulkes* or *tallits*," he added. "But I certainly talk about the feasts of Israel and show how they were fulfilled in Jesus. And I stress the wonderful Jewish culture and history to show how God has preserved us."

When I asked him how many Jewish people attend his congregation, he answered, "About forty percent of the congregation is Jewish."

Messianic Judaism Is Not the Answer

While I have no statistical evidence to support this next statement, I believe it to be true: If you asked a hundred Gentiles who attend Messianic congregations why they do so, or if you asked a hundred Jewish believers why they do not do so, their answers would probably be similar to the ones listed above.

The testimonies, evidence and experiences I have shared with you have helped to form my reaction to Messianic Judaism. But they are not the only—or the most important—bases for my beliefs. As we move into the next chapter and consider how Gentile and Jewish believers are to live their lives together, let us look to the only true source of all answers—God's Word.

7

ONE NEW MAN

A few years ago I was asked to speak at the Sixth International Conference of the Lausanne Consultation on Jewish Evangelism meeting in New York City. LCJE is made up of people from all over the world who are committed to the priority of reaching Jewish people with the Gospel. My assigned topic was "Trusting My Jewish Savior." In that message, I stressed that while before I was saved my identity was in the fact that I was Jewish, now that I am saved my identity is in Messiah Jesus. The Bible tells me that I am complete in Him. Of course, I am still Jewish and still a man and still an American, but my spiritual identity is now in Him and not in rabbinic Judaism.

I stressed that I did not have to prove to anyone that I was Jewish—not to the rabbinate, not to my friends and neighbors, not to the Jewish community, not to the Church and certainly not to other Jewish believers. I *am* a Jew.

I also stressed there, as I have stressed in this book, that following rabbinic and synagogal form does not make anyone Jewish any more than not following rabbinic or synagogal form takes away a Jewish person's identity. I did not do anything to become Jewish, and for the first fifty years of my life, I did not have to do anything to maintain my Jewish identity. God gave me a Jewish identity when He chose me to be born of Jewish parents. He reinforced my identity when He chose me to be born again by His Spirit, after I accepted Jesus as Israel's Messiah—and my personal Lord and Savior.

The message I shared at LCJE seemed to be well received by most of the people who attended that meeting. But some were present who were extremely involved in Messianic Judaism. They were upset by what I said, feeling that I was speaking against them. And our fellowship became strained!

From their reactions, I was reminded of three important truths: (1) I was to always seek to speak positively; (2) man learns best from reasons that he himself discovers; and (3) if you want to spot a counterfeit twenty-dollar bill, you do not spend your time studying the counterfeit. You study the original.

Accordingly, I want to write positively about what I myself discovered as I prayerfully studied the original word—the Word of God—on the subject of "one new man."

Second Corinthians: A New Creation

As an introduction for what is to follow, let me take you back to the fall of 1975, soon after I became a believer. I was studying 2 Corinthians 5:16–17. I remember underlining these verses: "So from now on we regard no one from a worldly point of view. Though we once regarded Christ in this way, we do so no longer. Therefore, if anyone is in Christ, he is a new creation; the old has gone, the new has come!"

I was challenged by both of those statements. I had been conditioned to *always* judge people from my worldly point of view: Were they Jewish? What was their education? Where did they live? What did they do for a living?

And verse 17 struck me as odd, too. I was not sure I understood what becoming a "new creation" meant.

To help me better understand what I was reading, I went to a Christian bookstore and talked to the store manager. When he understood my dilemma, he suggested that I get copies of Strong's concordance, the Amplified Bible and Matthew Henry's commentaries. I bought them all.

When I returned home, I opened *Strong's* and looked up the word *new* as used in 2 Corinthians 5:17. Here I found the Greek word *kainos*, which does not mean "next in number." It means entirely new, such as never existed before.

Then I looked up these verses in the Amplified translation and read this:

> Consequently, from now on we estimate and regard no one from a [purely] human point of view [in terms of natural standards of value]. [No] even though we once did estimate Christ from a human viewpoint and as a man, yet now [we have such knowledge of Him that] we know Him no longer [in terms of the flesh]. Therefore, if any person is [ingrafted] in Christ (the Messiah) he is a new creation (a new creature altogether); the old [previous moral and spiritual condition] has passed away. Behold, the fresh and new has come.

Matthew Henry's comments on verse 17 read: "The renewed man acts upon new principles, by new rules, with new ends and in new company. The believer is created anew; his heart is not merely set right, but a new heart is given him. He is the workmanship of God, created in Christ Jesus unto good works."

It took some doing, but as I continued to study, I remember saying to myself, *This means that each and every one of us who is born again is included in this "new creation" reality.*

As a Jew who loves being Jewish, I found this both fascinating and disturbing. What I was reading seemed to be saying that my Jewishness did not matter to God, and that other believers' Gentileness did not matter to God. In God's sight we were equally new creations. I remember scratching my head and repeating: *No matter whether we are Jews or Gentiles; no matter our race, color or nationality; no matter our education; no matter our social standing or our occupation—if Jesus is Lord of our lives, we are joined together spiritually as new creations.*

Galatians: You Are All One

As I continued to study, I found that statement echoed in Galatians 3:26–28: "You are all sons of God through faith in Christ Jesus, for all of you who were baptized into Christ have clothed yourselves with Christ. There is neither Jew nor Greek, slave nor free, male nor female, for you are all one in Christ Jesus." I remember stopping as I read these verses and saying to myself, *We are forgiven, liberated, united to the Messiah, yes—but how can we be de-Jewished or de-Americanized or de-socialized or de-genderized?*

I am sure you appreciate how hard it was for me to understand this statement. But then I read verse 29:

"If you belong to Christ, then you are Abraham's seed, and heirs according to the promise." As I thought about these verses I understood that, whether we are Jews or Gentiles, each believer in Jesus comes to God the same way—by faith. Though we may have different racial, cultural or ethnic roots, each of us has the same responsibilities on earth, and one day each of us will receive the same reward in heaven.

Then in Galatians 1:11–12, Paul stressed that the Gospel he was preaching did not come to him from men. It was revealed to him by God. This verse emphasized for me that much of what I was hearing in the Messianic synagogue I attended were the differing opinions and theories of *men* and not the Word of God.

When I really understood this truth, I began to look differently at myself and those around me. I began to see individual believers from what I perceived to be God's perspective of them. The more I did this, the more my heart was filled with confidence in God's Word.

Ephesians: One New Man

When I studied Ephesians for the first time, I noted that a key section (2:11–16) was clearly written to the Gentile believers in that city. After reviewing the universal scope of the Gospel, Paul in these eight verses wrote of the demand on all believers, Jews and Gentiles, to activate the "one new man" that God had produced in us:

Therefore, remember that formerly you who are Gentiles by birth and called "uncircumcised" by those who call themselves "the circumcision" (that done in the body by the hands of men)—remember that at that time you were separate from Christ, excluded from citizenship in Israel and foreigners to the covenants of the promise, without hope and without God in the world. But now in Christ Jesus you who once were far away have been brought near through the blood of Christ. For he himself is our peace, who has made the two one and has destroyed the barrier, the dividing wall of hostility, by abolishing in his flesh the law with its commandments and regulations. His purpose was to create in himself *one new man* out of the two, thus making peace, and in this one body to reconcile both of them to God through the cross, by which *he put to death their hostility* (emphasis mine).

I thought about these verses for quite a while. It was then that I highlighted Paul's statement in Ephesians 3:4–6:

In reading this, then, you will be able to understand my insight into the mystery of Christ, which was not made known to men in other generations as it has now been revealed by the Spirit to God's holy apostles and prophets. This mystery is that through the gospel the Gentiles are heirs together with Israel, members together of one body, and sharers together in the promise in Christ Jesus.

Then I read Ephesians 4:1–6:

As a prisoner for the Lord, then, I urge you to live a life worthy of the calling you have received. Be completely humble and gentle; be patient, bearing with one another in love. Make every effort to keep the unity of the Spirit through the bond of peace. There is one body and one Spirit—just as you were called to one hope when you were called—one Lord, one faith, one baptism; one God and Father of all, who is over all and through all and in all.

A little further on, in 4:12–14, I found myself focusing on the purpose of the fivefold ministry gifts: (1) to work together; (2) "to prepare God's people for works of service, so that the body of Christ may be built up"; (3) to "reach unity in the faith and in the knowledge of the Son of God and become mature"; (4) to attain "to the whole measure of the fullness of Christ"; (5) so that "we will no longer be infants, tossed back and forth by the waves, and blown here and there by every wind of teaching and by the cunning and craftiness of men in their deceitful scheming."

When I thought about what I had read in verse 14, I realized that in many ways I had become confused by the different winds of doctrine that were being proclaimed by certain leaders in Messianic Judaism. I also realized that I was not the only Jewish believer who felt this way. I was beginning to find that all too many, like myself, were similarly confused. Why? Because we were being encouraged to follow the teachings of men rather than the Word of God. Why was that? Because our leaders did not stress or demand our full submission to God's Word. Instead they seemed to be trying to gain the acceptance of the rabbis and of the Jewish establishment.

But God does not call us to compromise truth. He appeals to our spirits to do His will and *not* compromise His truth.

Summing It Up

From the Scriptures I have reviewed, we can conclude the following: Upon receiving Messiah Jesus as our Lord and Savior, we are created anew. This means that each and every one of us—Jew and Gentile alike—is now a completely new being, such as never existed before. We are no longer to be separated as Jews or Gentiles, for we are all one in the Lord. Through His redeeming work on the cross, He has removed the barriers between us and created one new man out of the two. We are

We are no longer to be separated as Jews or Gentiles, for we are all one in the Lord.

heirs together, members of one Body, sharers in the promise of Messiah Jesus. Though we have different racial, cultural and ethnic roots, we are now called to one Body, one Lord, one faith, one purpose, one baptism and one hope.

How We Are to Live

As this "one new man," we have specific work to do! And Messiah Jesus is to be our model. According to God's Word, our present objective is to grow and become more like Jesus, so that with His leading and empowerment we will be ready, willing and able to do what He has called us to do.

Jesus said, "All authority in heaven and on earth has been given to me. Therefore go and make disciples of all nations" (Matthew 28:18–19). When I read the word *disciple*, I think of the word *understudy*. The understudy prepares himself to play the role when the principal actor cannot go on. Is that not what Jesus said we are to do? Did He not say, "Anyone who has faith in me will do what I have been doing. He will do even greater things than these" (John 14:12)?

Ephesians 4:22–24 also tells us how to live. This passage says to put off the old self, which is being corrupted by its deceitful desires, to submit to becoming new in the attitude of our minds and finally to put on the new self, which is created to be like God in true righteousness and holiness. It is significant that verse 29 adds: "Do not let any unwholesome talk come out of your mouths, but only what is helpful for building others up according to their needs, that it may benefit

94

those who listen." As new men and part of one Body, this is how we are to act.

And what shall I say about the wonderful prayer of Jesus in John 17? At verse 20, He prayed: "My prayer is not for them alone. I pray also for those who will believe in me through their message, that all of them may be one, Father, just as you are in me and I am in you. May they also be in us so that the world may believe that you have sent me." We must underscore the importance of God's concern—that it is now possible for redeemed Jews and Gentiles to be completely reconciled and completely fused into the "one new man." When the reality of this statement is visible in our lives, the world will know that the Father sent Jesus to earth.

Throughout the New Covenant we see that our focus is not to be on us! It is to be on Him! We are to be increasingly transformed into *His* image! Since we have been directed to represent *Him* to the world, we must exhibit *His* righteousness. We are to manifest and exhibit His character to all who have eyes to see! As 1 Corinthians 10:31 specifically tells us, "Whether you eat or drink or whatever you do, *do it all for the glory of God!*" (emphasis mine).

Our purpose as "one new man" is not to please man. We are to please only God! We are to be who God says we are. And we are to live our lives in accordance with His Word. We are to live as His "one new man." We are to be unlike any men who have ever lived before—unlike any other Jewish people and unlike any other Gentile people.

Jesus never compromised truth. He was not concerned about what the Jewish community or the Jewish leadership thought. He was concerned exclusively with God's concerns—with what God decreed in His Word. And we who believe are to have the same concerns.

Applying God's Word to Messianic Judaism

I trust you will agree that any undue emphasis by men based on ethnicity, on a particular worldly heritage or on form or day of worship—any one of which causing us to be divided—is contrary to the will of God. To emphasize the point I want to make, let me ask this: Have you noticed that as long as we are reading or speaking from God's Word, a sense of peace fills our spirits? But when we give undue emphasis to ethnicity . . . or calling . . . or personal heritage . . . or form of worship, then heat rises within us and we lose our peace.

Keeping in mind, then, that we are to be united and not divided, let us look at how God's Word—rather than the undue emphasis of men—applies to Messianic Judaism. I do this reluctantly and with deep humility because of my love for my brothers and sisters who are in the movement.

But first, I must again remind you that there are innumerable factions within Jewish ministry, and what I am about to say will not apply to each of them. Please prayerfully and carefully consider the following comments.

How Messianic Judaism Turned from God's Word

For many decades now, some able and committed Jewish believers have struggled with two serious questions: "How are we to live our lives as Jewish believers?" and "How are we to prove that, even though we believe in Jesus, we are still Jewish?"

Because of the anti-Semitism within the Church—whether historical, traditional or contemporary—you certainly can understand why these questions were asked. But I stress to you and to those who asked these questions that they were asking the wrong questions. And so they received the wrong answers!

Instead of looking to the Word of God for instruction about how we are to live our lives and bring glory to His name, many Jewish believers have fallen into the trap of becoming preoccupied with themselves and with their separate ministries. They also have set out to prove to the rabbis, to the Jewish community and perhaps even to themselves that—even though they believe in Jesus—*they are still Jewish!*

Prove what? To whom? Why?

Soon some wonderful Gentile believers who also wanted to reach Jewish people joined them. Together they began to search for ways to accomplish both objectives. And as I have previously stressed, while there is great depth to Jewish life and culture, the areas on which they chose to concentrate were rabbinic practice and synagogal form.

Then they developed a "movement" and "practices" to demonstrate what they felt was "Jewishness." Later they began to judge the practices of others: This congregation was "more Jewish." . . . That one was "more Torah observant." . . . Another had "more Jewish members." . . . In another "more people kept kosher." . . . Yet another had better music and "Davidic" dancing! All of these things seemed to help them answer the question about how they were to maintain their "Jewishness" now that they were believers in Jesus as the Messiah.

Now please consider: Is there any place in Scripture where God directs us Jews to "prove our Jewishness"? Is there any place where He directs Gentiles to "prove their Jewishness"? Does concentrating on rabbinic form bring glory to God? Does rabbinic form equip us to do what Jesus did? Does it help us to develop more understudies of Messiah Jesus? Will focusing on our "Jewishness" in our worship help us reach more Jewish people with the

97

Gospel? Has it done so in the past? Do we not understand that currently only seven percent of the Jewish people in the United States attend a synagogue as often as twice a month? Do we not also understand that at least 85 percent of the Jewish people in the world are secular? Do we admit that the overwhelming majority of people who attend Messianic synagogues in the United States *are not Jewish*?

I say again that God does not direct Jews—and certainly does not direct Gentiles—to prove their "Jewishness." He calls us to represent Him as one new man. As those in the Messianic movement stress their "Jewishness," they separate themselves from the rest of the Body of Christ. Instead of being united by the Holy Spirit in love, believers are being divided into camps or movements by the rabbinic practices they choose to emphasize—or by the leaders they choose to follow. And the unity that God desires for us all continues to be broken.

> *Scripture clearly establishes the fact that God does not want those ethnic and cultural differences to divide us. He wants us to be united.*

Endless debates go on as the proponents of Messianic Judaism keep asking the two wrong questions I mentioned above—the questions that really started the movement: "How are we to live our lives as Jewish believers?" and "How are we to prove that, even though we believe in Jesus, we are still Jewish?" As a result of these debates, the continually changing winds of doctrine keep blowing . . . and blowing . . . and blowing . . . and many of God's children are increasingly tossed to and fro, losing their peace—and their witness—and withdrawing further and further from the rest of God's family.

No Longer Jews?

Does this mean, then, that Jewish believers must no longer live as Jews? Are we Jewish believers to be prohibited from *culturally* identifying ourselves as Jews? Are we supposed to forget our Jewish heritage and culture?

Or is my wife, who is of Syrian Arab descent, to stop cooking Arabic food or enjoying Arabic music? Is a dear friend of mine, who was a Greek Orthodox priest before he got saved, to stop enjoying Greek food or his Greek culture, or relating to others of Greek descent? Or does anyone have the right to insist that Muslim men who become believers still have to pray on their mats five times each day in order to relate to other Muslims?

Of course not!

Let me make this next point crystal clear: I am not opposed to any ethnic group of people articulating its social, moral and cultural heritage. When we become believers, we do not turn our backs on whom God made us to be.

But Scripture clearly establishes the fact that God does not want those ethnic and cultural differences to divide us. He wants us to be united. No matter what our culture or heritage, we are to be one new man in Messiah Jesus. And God's will is that as "one new man" we go from Jerusalem to Judea to Samaria and to the uttermost parts of the world making disciples of *all* nations. To the Jew first, and also to the Gentile! That is our mission.

God's Will for Us

What we have seen occur within the Messianic movement is a most tragic shift in purpose. Where the original emphasis of the movement was to share the Gospel with

Jewish people, the present purpose appears to be the protection of their now enshrined—and institutionalized—doctrine and rituals.

But God does not want us to enshrine and institutionalize our doctrine and rituals. And He does not want us to look to the changing philosophies of men. He wants us to look to His unchanging Word for our direction and our practices. He wants us to see ourselves the way He sees us. He wants us to see ourselves as one new man who has been called to reveal His love and His character as we share His Gospel to all who have ears to hear—to the Jew first and also to the Gentile.

That is *God's* will for us. What, then, will be our will for us? As we think about this question, we should recall Isaiah 30:8, which says:

> The Lord told me to write down His message for His people, so that it would be there forever. They turned against the Lord and cannot be trusted. They have refused His teaching and have said to His messengers and prophets: Don't tell us what God has shown you and don't preach the truth. Just say what we want to hear, even if it is false. Stop telling us what God has said.
>
> CEV

I pray that this will not be the response of Jewish or Gentile participants in Messianic Judaism.

8

HOW JEWISH PEOPLE
ARE BEING REACHED

Before we review how Jewish people *are* being reached with the Gospel, let us look at how they are not being reached by the Messianic movement.

Messianic Leaders Agree

I want you to read what David Sedaca, one of the leaders in the Messianic movement, had to say about the outreach effectiveness of the Messianic Jewish congregations. He wrote, "Congregations have not obtained the level of success in reaching out to the Jews that they could have. In a way, it seems to attract more Gentiles who are drawn toward Messianic worship and lifestyle than it attracts traditional Jews. Nevertheless, as it was in the early Church, it seems logical that Jewish outreach ought to be the primary endeavor of the Messianic Jewish congregation."[1]

Sedaca then listed four possible reasons why Messianic Jewish congregations are not carrying out Jewish evangelism to the fullest potential:

1. One of the main reasons for the existence of the Messianic Jewish congregations is to identify themselves with the Jewish community. While this in itself is a worthy cause, it has had as collateral effect the reluctance to promote evangelism. The congregation is always careful not to do or say anything that might endanger its relationship with the outside Jewish community.

2. Similar but not equal is the reluctance of the Messianic Jewish congregation to promote any event or program that might be misunderstood by the outside Jewish community as doing "missionary" work or proselytizing. The overriding fear is that if the congregation is viewed as a "missionary" agent, it might forfeit its chances to win acceptance into the Jewish community.

3. Typically, the Messianic Jewish congregation has a particular worship style. The combination of Jewish worship, Israeli folklore and a strong spiritual content resulted in what is known as *Davidic praise and worship.* Its vitality and spirituality made it the heart of the worship service. But a strong emphasis on praise and worship practices subordinates the core of the congregation's beliefs as to how these beliefs are expressed. A case in point is the fact that the Messianic Jewish congregations will frequently feature and promote Messianic musicians and dance groups, while one rarely sees the setting up of a special program to hear a Jewish evangelist.

4. With some exceptions, today Messianic leaders lack the necessary training to carry out Jewish evangelism efficiently. This was not the case at the beginning of the Messianic movement, when most leaders were part of or came from Jewish missions.[2]

Another leader in the movement said this: "The UMJC [Union of Messianic Jewish Congregations] does not missionize. . . . We do not hand out pamphlets. We have no association with Jews for Jesus, who have an entirely different mentality, outlook and starting point."[3]

The above statements should stun you. If a Messianic congregation—or indeed any congregation—is to be biblically sound, it must follow the biblical mandate to share the Gospel with all who have ears to hear, including the Jewish people.

David Stern, writing from Israel, agrees and says very clearly: "Let me say at the outset that evangelism is not an option, but a command. A believer who does not communicate the Gospel to unbelievers is not only sinning against love of his fellow human beings by withholding the means of eternal life but is also refusing to obey Yeshua's order to go into all the world and make disciples. Moreover, doing evangelism is one of God's ways of blessing a believer—the reward is the act itself."[4]

Sedaca also made this important observation: "The congregation needs to be recognized by its beliefs, not by its worship style. What it believes and stands for needs to be more important than how these beliefs are expressed."[5]

As one who holds an international office and is deeply involved with the Messianic movement, Sedaca has made some powerful statements. He clearly suggests that Messianic congregations have not been effective in reaching Jewish people with the Gospel. They have allowed their desire to receive favor from the Jewish community to dull their obedience to God's Great Commission. Their hearts are divided.

Winning Acceptance?

This desire for acceptance, however, will not happen unless the Lord intervenes. Having lived my life in and having been part of the Jewish community for, lo, these many years, I am able to say to you that Messianic Judaism will never succeed in winning acceptance by the traditional Jewish community. William Varner, Arnold Fruchtenbaum and others all agree that "Messianic Jews will never be able to please Jewish religious leaders today, no matter how 'Jewish' they try to be."[6]

Why do we say that? Are you familiar with the statement that "individuals are expendable; the institution must survive"? That could well have been the battle cry of the Pharisees during Jesus' day. Today the institution of Judaism has as one of its foundational principles that Jesus is not the Messiah. We disagree. Now, if we are right, it is wrong. And short of the Second Coming of the Messiah, I cannot envision its ever admitting it is wrong. That is not what institutions do. So the mission of the Messianic movement to win favor from the Jewish community is doomed to failure. Will they ever see it? I am not sure.

How Jewish People *Are* Being Reached

In my book *Abandoned*, I quoted statistics from a survey done by Jews for Jesus in the 1990s.[7] To the best of my knowledge this is the latest survey available. With the gracious permission of Jews for Jesus, I retained someone to review the survey they had made. She reviewed 1,187 of the 4,500 responses to the question, "While you were yet an unbeliever, what first attracted you to consider the Gospel?" Here is what the survey revealed:

Response	Number	Percentage
Christian friends	332	28%
Jesus Christ/ Holy Spirit	134	11%
A believing relative	113	10%
A life crisis	111	9%
Bible/Gospel	83	7%
A mixed marriage	53	4%
A vision/feeling/ supernatural dream/ miracle	39	3%
A pastor	39	3%
General search	36	3%
Friends who seemed at peace	21	2%
Messianic prophecies	17	1%
TV evangelists/radio shows	17	1%
Curiosity	17	1%
A book	16	1%
Jews for Jesus	16	1%
Billy Graham	12	1%
Old Testament study	11	1%
Searching for Jewish roots	10	1%
Miscellaneous other attractions	110	9%
(Fewer than 10 in each category)		

I remember realizing that there is no way of getting away from it: In addition to the power of the Holy Spirit, the primary initial attraction came from believing friends and relatives. Something in their lives attracted the responders enough that they were willing to listen as the Gospel was presented. Surely you can now see that we Jews are just like everybody else: Though we often resemble other Jews on the outside, we are very different on the inside. There is no one formula, method, ministry or technique that can attract all Jews to the Gospel. With that thought clearly established, we are ready to consider the next survey.

What Helped You Decide to Accept Jesus?

In 1996 I contacted a thousand Jewish believers and asked them to answer this question: "What was the one (or two) most important factor(s) in your coming to the Lord?"

The direct mail industry observes that when one sends out a mailing piece it is normal to receive about a one percent response. My questionnaire produced a seven percent response. Some of the responders listed more than one important factor that helped them come to the Lord. Here is what the survey revealed:

Response	Number	Percentage
Study of the Bible	42	39.6%
Testimony of believing friends	33	31.1%
Testimony of saved relatives	10	9.4%
Preaching of Gospel by a minister	8	7.5%
Prayers of the saints	7	6.6%
Other	6	5.7%

Though this survey was modest, it again revealed the truth that "the Gospel is the power of God unto salvation for all who believe, for the Jew first and also for the Gentile" (Romans 1:16, CEV). Most often the Gospel is revealed to a person while reading Scripture. At other times it is revealed as God's witnesses share their testimony. And did you notice that none of the responders mentioned "Jewishness" as the thing that first attracted them to the Messiah, or that it was the key factor in their accepting the Lord?

Let's examine some of the statements I received in more detail.

Reading the Bible

Bob, who has been a believer for more than thirty years, described how reading the Bible is what brought him to the Lord: "It was 1971. I was nineteen and looking for meaning and relevance. Jesus was the preeminent hippie—that is what I read in the New Testament! Reading that Book is the number-one reason I am saved."

> *None of the responders mentioned "Jewishness" as the thing that first attracted them to the Messiah.*

Lisa, who has been saved for four years, said the same thing:

Reading the Bible was by far the most influential factor in my coming to the Lord. As I began to read, I found I had numerous misconceptions about what Judaism and Jewish history were all about. At first I felt completely lost and had many questions, which I wrote down in my journal. Gradually, as I read on, I began to grasp many basic concepts, and my understanding deepened. The more I studied the Bible, the more I saw Jesus' life prophesied in the Old Testament. I read the Old and the New Testaments over the course of a year.

After the first three months, I became convinced that Jesus was the Messiah, and as I continued in my studies my convictions deepened. I know that my decision to come to the Lord was strictly between myself and God. I am certain that the foundation of my faith is rooted solidly in the Word of God and not in anything any human has told me. I knew I still had my doubts, fears and concerns, but I also knew I could trust God to show me the truth, as He had in the past.

Marilyn, who has been a believer for seven years, echoed their experiences:

> When I turned thirty, my husband and I decided to start a family. At that time I began to think about which religion I would raise my child in. I was raised as a Conservative Jew, and my husband was a non-practicing Presbyterian. I began to feel that there was a God who cared about me, and I had a desire to search for a way to reach Him. I began to attend various churches, including a Unitarian church, a sort of New Age cult and just about every denomination. I even went to an astrologer and practiced meditation. I continued to feel emptiness and a longing to know God.
>
> It was not until my sister-in-law, who is a born-again Christian, left a Bible at my house that I began to get the answers I so desperately needed. When I read the prophecies in the Old Testament and how they were fulfilled by Jesus Christ, I was totally amazed. A few days later I received Jesus as my personal Messiah and began my walk with the Lord.
>
> I thank God every day for giving me the desire in my heart to know Him, and for my sister-in-law, who provided me with God's Word.

And Barb, a believer for thirteen years, said, "The love that was shown to me and that was so evident about me in the churches I visited provoked me to jealousy. I wanted what they had. I never found it in the synagogues I had attended and where I had been very active."

Scripture Plus Personal Assurances

Lorie, who had been saved for three-and-a-half years when she responded to my survey, wrote me a long letter. In part she wrote:

Over nine years I studied Scripture on and off. And I began to think about my own mortality. Did I want to go to the grave thinking that a dark hole was all that awaited me? Fear ripped through me, and an equally strong thought raced around my head: I needed to believe in God.

Time continued to pass. Then one day:

I passed by a local church and something inside me said, "Check this out." I went in soon after. The pastor there, an exceptional expository preacher, led a congregation of warm, friendly, Bible-believing people. Then came the invitation. By this point I had grown to believe that Yeshua was most likely the Messiah, but I was having trouble accepting Him as the Son of God. I kept fearing that God would be so terribly angry at me for breaking the second commandment about not worshipping false gods. Suddenly I felt my feet moving. Too shocked at this event, I clung to the chair in front of me. No! I was a Jew, and I was not going to walk down that aisle.

An almost uncomfortable blast of adrenaline shot through me, but I clung tight and eventually left the building. But it made me think of the Scripture I had been hearing or reading repeatedly over those previous weeks—the one that said Yeshua would keep on knocking, but if we hardened our hearts too much He would eventually leave us alone and we would never become part of the family of God. Terrified that this might happen, I invited the pastor over for a talk.

My main concern was for the pastor to reassure me that he would continue to view me as a Jewish believer. I did not view myself as a "convert" or as having changed faiths. I merely saw it as an enhancement of my own. He provided me with that assurance prior to leading me in the sinner's prayer.

The Preaching of an Anointed Minister

When he responded to my survey, Mark had been a believer for six years. Here is how he answered my question:

> First I was struck by the realization that my way was not working anymore. No matter how hard I tried to make things right, my desperation grew deeper and deeper. I was invited to a church service and went in without any preconceived ideas. The Holy Spirit touched my heart and began working in my life.
>
> Second, once I decided to look into Christianity and try to figure out who or what Jesus is, the Lord made Christians available to answer my many questions.
>
> The most important realization I had was: The fact that I am Jewish did not mean I could not follow the Lord.

Three Separate Factors

Sue has been a Jewish believer for sixteen years. She lists three factors that helped her come to faith: "First, believers loving me and praying for my salvation. Second, reading both Testaments as one book and finding that the New Testament answers the prophetic questions raised in the Old Testament regarding the Messiah and other issues. And third, my own search for truth and meaning. I was hungry and thirsty and broken, and the Lord found and met my every need."

The Lightbulb Phenomenon

When he responded to the survey, Mason had been a believer for only six months. He stated:

Two deciding factors "pushed me over the edge" to accepting Jesus as the Messiah. One was realizing that God does not operate the way I want Him to, and that in order to have a relationship with Him it would have to be on His terms, rather than my own. I also realized that there is always a price to forgiveness, and that there can be no true forgiveness without one side bearing its cost.

Initially the concept of sin was difficult to accept. I gradually began to see, however, that there was no means by which I could through my own good works be unconditionally right and acceptable with a perfect and holy God.

Provoke Them to Jealousy

Clearly these responses reinforce our observation that different people are reached in different ways. Yet underlying almost all of the responses is the powerful truth of Paul's instructions: The Jewish people are to be "provoked to jealousy" (see Romans 11:11). Certainly the Jewish people quoted above were provoked to jealousy by what they saw in the lives of their friends and relatives, what they read in Scripture and what they heard from the pulpit.

> The Jewish people are to be "provoked to jealousy."

What a clear reminder this is that it is not our ability that saves anyone. The Gospel is and always will be the power of God unto salvation for all who believe—for the Jew first and also for the Gentile (see Romans 1:16).

And that is certainly true in Israel. Let's look there next.

9

WHAT ABOUT CONGREGATIONS IN ISRAEL?

Despite the terrible ordeals Israel has experienced in recent years, the Gospel is being preached and the Church is growing.

Growth and Subsequent Challenges

In 1997 it was estimated that there were approximately six thousand Jewish believers in Israel with more than 85 congregations to serve them. Since then the number has grown to over ten thousand believers and more than two hundred congregations. Lisa Loden, in a paper delivered in August 2003 at the Seventh International Conference of the Lausanne Consultation on Jewish Evangelism in Helsinki, Finland, reported that this growth came about for two important reasons:

first, the great evangelistic enthusiasm of the Jewish believers who came to the Lord in the past five years; and second, the large influx to Israel of Russian Jews who were already believers.

As you would expect, with this substantial growth came many problems. Pastors had to be trained and leadership developed. Because of the serous lack of Bible schools and seminaries in Israel, this problem was acute. Indeed, many of the new leaders still do not have any theological education and training. Additionally, there is a serious lack of Christian literature in Hebrew.

Lisa Loden said:

> In general, there is little theological reflection, and where there are critical issues, they are frequently laid aside in the press of the practical. There are no forums or discussion group meetings on an ongoing basis to reflect and discuss theological issues. The community is focused on activity and seems not to have time for, or not to see, the importance of long-term reasoned theological reflection. Differences are not openly discussed and worked through, and the tendency is to fellowship with those who are most like you, to avoid groups with whom you may differ and to indulge in polemic name-calling from a safe distance.[1]

This is not to say that the Messianic community has not seen any spiritual growth or that practical matters are not being addressed. Indeed, many ministries and outreach programs have been formed to meet the acute social needs in the country. I am told that there are more than a dozen active centers ministering to the practical needs of the homeless, the elderly and the infirm, as well as a pro-life center and a counseling ministry that seeks to meet the psychological needs of congregation members.

Additionally, to meet the needs of the Russian immigrants, a large number of Russian-speaking leaders have emerged, and many new congregations have been formed. But again, I point out that the lack of seminaries, Bible schools and Christian literature in Hebrew continues to hamper the new leaders and congregation members.

Other Pressures

Arthur Goldberg, the LCJE coordinator for Israel, described a different set of problems facing Jewish believers in Israel. He said:

> We face pressures as a Messianic community from certain Israeli government offices and private anti-missionary groups, but the greatest obstacles to evangelism in Israel often come from within. We need to present a united front. We need a unity that crosses over all the defensive barriers, so we can agree to reach out and share Yeshua with our people. We are too often totally absorbed and preoccupied with our own agendas to the complete exclusion of the only real need of the nation of Israel and our Jewish people: Yeshua.[2]

One cause of the lack of unity is that some Jewish believers in Israel question the deity of Jesus. While the group is small, this issue has generated considerable heat because it is such a foundational one. Speaking about this problem, Lisa Loden wrote, "The more mature believers in Israel are attempting to deal with this issue while maintaining the unity of the Body. In 2002 at a national pastors' conference, eighty pastors were present. All but two of them affirmed the deity of Jesus."[3]

115

Superimposing Cultures?

Kai Kjaer-Hansen and Bodil F. Skjøtt wrote an informative book called *Facts and Myths about the Messianic Congregations in Israel.*[4] In it they reported a survey they conducted in 1998–99 of 81 congregations. Nine of these congregations were different from the other 72. While they could not really be called "Messianic congregations" and be compared to those congregations practicing "Messianic Judaism" in the United States, they do affirm that a "Jewish flavor" in a congregation is not enough. For the majority of these nine congregations, it is important to "practice Jewish traditions" as long as they do not contradict the Gospel.

> Most American Jews are assimilated and outwardly indistinguishable from American Gentiles.

They affirm that an identifiable Jewish lifestyle as a testimony to the Jewish people is central to their practice even as they also affirm the unity of Jews and Gentiles in the Body of Messiah.

Clearly they are affirming the importance of Jewish culture for Jewish believers in Israel. And surely we can understand that. But let's expand that thought and consider the cultural aspects of life in other nations. Just as you cannot superimpose a Korean culture on a church you plant in Norway, so an Israeli Jewish culture cannot be superimposed on believers in other lands. The church has to reflect the culture of its people. Applying that thought, we must observe that the Jewish culture in America is extremely diverse. Additionally, most American Jews are assimilated and outwardly indistinguishable from American Gentiles.

An Amusing Story

Rivka, a Jewish believer in Israel, shared an amusing story with me. I think you will enjoy it. She wrote:

> For the longest time I kept getting e-mails from a friend of mine in the States who repeatedly asked me if I attend a Messianic congregation. Each time I would write back to her and say, "I live in Israel—of course I attend a Messianic congregation!" It was only after I learned more about the problem of Messianic Judaism in the States that I understood her question. She was asking, "Do you attend a Messianic synagogue like they have in the United States?" My answer to her was, no, I do not.

Rivka's friend could also have asked, "Are you a Messianic Jew or a Jewish Christian?" And Rivka's answer would probably have been "yes." You see, in Hebrew the identical words are used to describe a "Messianic Jew" and "Jewish Christian." What is more, the Hebrew term *meshichi* is also used to describe non-Jewish believers in traditional evangelical churches, so that it is equivalent to the English word *evangelical*.

Rabbinic Form in Israeli Congregations

It is important to note that the rabbinic form that characterizes so many congregations involved in Messianic Judaism in the United States is not present in Israeli Messianic congregations. Speaking to this point, Kai Kjaer-Hansen explains:

> None call themselves synagogue, and none of the leaders call themselves rabbi. . . . In other words, the North American Messianic movement has had only a modest impact on the Messianic congregations in Israel. . . . Gen-

117

erally speaking, there is a vision of the "one new man" of Ephesians 2, constituted by Jews and Gentiles.

It would be wrong to say that the question of Jewish identity is irrelevant in these congregations, but it does not have the same weight as in the above-mentioned congregations. And generally speaking, they do not feel the same need to disassociate themselves from the Christian church.[5]

Messianic Judaism of Little Interest in Israel

What you must certainly have observed from these comments is that Messianic Judaism is of little interest to Jewish believers in Israel. Although a number of American leaders in the Messianic movement have emigrated to Israel and have attempted to create American-style Messianic synagogues, they have not succeeded in doing so.

A Critical Observation

And now we come to a very important point. In the second and third centuries, it became clear to the rabbis that faith in Jesus as Messiah contradicted continued reliance on the Torah for right standing with God. Speaking to this point and referring to the first-century Jewish Church, Baruch Maoz wrote:

(Rabbinic) practice was, in fact, contradicted by their faith in Jesus, and the rabbis were quicker to recognize this than was the early Church. Rabbinicism recognizes an incipient, inevitable contradiction between practicing the Torah and seeking to combine such practice with any kind of religious faith in Jesus. In that sense, rabbinicism is more biblical than modern-day adherents to

118

WHAT ABOUT CONGREGATIONS IN ISRAEL?

Messianic Judaism. The adherents of that movement are
blind to the contradiction because they are so focused
on being recognized as Jewish that they have failed to
reflect sufficiently on the greatness and the finality of
the Person and work of Jesus.[6]

If you stop to think about this key point, you can understand why the rabbis today refuse to recognize the
legitimacy of Messianic Judaism. And they doubt the
integrity of Messianic Jews who declare both a belief in
Jesus as Messiah and Lord and their faith in the practice
of rabbinic Judaism. Again and again they repeat, "You
cannot be Jewish if you believe in Jesus."

What Will Be the Result?

Baruch Maoz declares:

> If being accepted by the Jewish people is the major issue,
> Messianic Jews will have no choice but to continually
> erode their biblical convictions concerning Jesus until
> they finally turn their back to Messiah and embrace a
> wholly rabbinic Judaism. It is a matter of grave concern
> to note that such tendencies are increasingly evident
> among some Messianic Jewish groups.[7]

I could not agree more with Maoz's quote. As I have
observed Messianic Judaism in the United States over
the years, I have seen an increasing emphasis on being
"accepted" by the Jewish community and an increased
reliance on rabbinic form as the means to achieve that
objective.

Is it working? In the fall of 2003, I was invited to participate in a debate on a TV talk show. I was partnered
with Andrew, another Jewish believer. Our opponents,
whom I will call "Tamara" and "Murray," were two

prominent people from the Jewish community who did not believe in Jesus. As the sixty-minute program continued, the emotional intensity of the comments from Tamara and Murray increased. Murray insisted that Andrew and I were no longer Jews but had become Christians. He refused to consider the possibility that one could be both. Obviously he was thinking that we had become Gentiles.

In the last few minutes of the broadcast, Tamara made a very emotional attack against us. She said that we were deceiving people by wearing skull caps and prayer shawls, the garments of observant Jews, and that we had no right to wear them. When I told her I wore neither and that she was using a very broad brush to attack all Jewish believers, she dismissed my comments and insisted that people who call themselves Jews and who believe in Jesus are deceivers. She said, "If you want to be Christians, be Christians, but don't pretend that you are Jews!"

Though Tamara and many others believe that statement to be true, it is absolutely incorrect. She was confusing ethnicity with belief. Let me explain.

God has decreed that there are two categories of people on earth. There are the descendants of Abraham, Isaac and Jacob—the Jewish people—and then there are all the people of the nations, usually referred to as Gentiles. If you are a descendant of Abraham, Isaac and Jacob, you cannot *not* be a descendant of Abraham, Isaac and Jacob. If you are Jewish, you cannot be a Gentile. And if you are a Gentile, you cannot be Jewish. (Though Gentiles can become proselytes to Judaism and their children will be considered Jewish.)

What Tamara was doing—and what many others often do—was substituting the word *Gentile* for the word *Christian*. To her thinking, therefore, one cannot be Jewish and a Christian at the same time. Obviously

Tamara's understanding is erroneous. All of the early "Christians" were Jewish, and throughout the centuries there have been Jewish Christians. Indeed it would be safe to say that Christians can be found in all ethnic groups. Unfortunately, I did not have an opportunity to discuss with Tamara the mistake she was making.

But the point is that Tamara clearly does not accept Messianic Judaism, and her comments are representative of the Jewish community as a whole.

10

IS MESSIANIC JUDAISM
GOD'S WAY?

In view of all we have considered thus far, we have to ask what role Messianic Judaism plays in God's plan for the Jewish people and the Church. In order to lay the groundwork, let us first look at what God's Word says about His will and plan for His chosen people.

God's Heart Attitude

Using God's Word as our guide, let us examine the question: "What is God's heart attitude toward the Jewish people?" I believe that Jeremiah 31:3–4 states it clearly: "The LORD appeared to us in the past, saying: 'I have loved you with an everlasting love; I have drawn you with loving-kindness. I will build you up again and you will be rebuilt, O Virgin Israel. Again

> **What is God's heart attitude toward the Jewish people?**

you will take up your tambourines and go out to dance with the joyful.'"

God's love for His covenant people will last forever. And they will exist as a nation before God as long as the sun comes up in the morning and the moon and stars come up at night (see Jeremiah 31:35–37).

Paul Sums Up God's Plan

And we must remember the critically important teachings of the apostle Paul in Romans 9, 10 and 11. In each of these chapters Paul expresses his personal identification with the people of Israel, but not without expressing his sorrow over their unbelief (chapter 9), his prayerful longing for their salvation (chapter 10) and his conviction that God has not rejected them (chapter 11). And then Paul boldly concludes that it is God's plan that one day all Israel will be saved! (See Romans 11:25–26.)

In chapter 11 Paul tells us of the three stages of the mystery of God's plan. First, the Jewish violations of God's covenant with them opened the way for the second stage, which was the salvation of Gentiles. This in turn leads to the third stage: the salvation of the Jewish people. This progression is so important to Paul that he restates it six times in this chapter (see verses 12, 15, 16, 17–24, 25–26, 30–32).

But it is not enough just to summarize these conclusions. We must carefully examine the text itself:

> So I ask, Have they stumbled so as to fall—to their utter spiritual ruin, irretrievably? By no means! But through their false step and transgression salvation

[has come] to the Gentiles, so as to arouse Israel [to see and feel what they forfeited] and so to make them jealous. Now if their stumbling—their lapse, their transgression—has so enriched the world [at large], and if [Israel's] failure means such riches for the Gentiles, think what an enrichment and greater advantage will follow their reinstatement!

Romans 11:11–12, AMP

The Olive Tree

Then, Paul's illustration of the olive tree emphasizes and repeats his conviction about God's plan for the Jewish people (see Romans 11:21). Here he reminds the Gentile believers of whose faith they have adopted. Paul declares that the Gentiles were grafted into the olive tree "contrary to nature," but Jews can be—and will be—grafted back into God's olive tree as natural branches once they come back to Him by faith (see verses 16–24). And if there was rejoicing over the fact that Gentiles were grafted in, can you imagine the overwhelming rejoicing there will be when the natural branches—the Jewish people—are grafted back in?

Then Paul makes this statement:

Lest you be self-opinionated—wise in your own conceits—I do not want you to miss this hidden truth and mystery, brethren: a hardening [insensibility] has [temporarily] befallen a part of Israel [to last] until the full number of the ingathering of the Gentiles has come in, And so all Israel will be saved. As it is written, The Deliverer will come from Zion, He will banish ungodliness from Jacob. And this will be My covenant—My agreement—with them when I shall take away their sins.

Romans 11:25–27, AMP

Paul explains:

> From the point of view of the Gospel [Good News] they [the Jews, at present] are enemies [of God], which is for your advantage and benefit. But from the point of view of God's choice—of election, of divine selection—they are still the beloved [dear to Him] for the sake of their forefathers. For God's gifts and His call are irrevocable—He never withdraws them when once they are given, and He does not change His mind about those to whom He gives His grace and to whom He sends His call.
>
> Romans 11:28–29, AMP

I think the point is clear: It is God's *will* that the Jewish people be restored to Him by faith.

Yes, but How Are They to Be Saved?

And how will God restore His chosen people to Himself? As we talked about briefly in chapter 8, God wants His Church to provoke Israel to jealousy (see Romans 11:11). How is this to be done? By works? Shall we run comparisons between the number of Nobel prizes Christians have won versus the number Jews have won? Shall we contrast Christian versus Jewish contributions to art, music, the sciences and philanthropy?

How will God restore His chosen people to Himself?

Provoking someone to jealousy is not a matter of stressing the externals of our lives—where we live or where we go to church or how much money we have or how successful we are. Nor is our Jewishness the primary issue. Paul knew by the power of the Holy Spirit that only when the Jewish people are jealous enough of *our relationship with God* and *with one another* will they forget their fears and prior conditioning and long for what the followers of Jesus have.

I believe Paul is stressing that we believers are to provoke the Jewish people to jealousy by revealing to them the difference Jesus has made in our lives. They need to see Jesus in us. They need to see that He is the hope of our glory! They need to see the love of God in us. Our daily lives must reveal the truth that only God makes possible our joy and our blessed hope. In fact, it is our very confidence in Him, our love, our unity, our obedience and the victory we experience in our lives that make us credible as we share our testimony with those who do not yet know Jesus. We are the message that our Jewish and non-Jewish friends, neighbors, classmates and co-workers must hear. And only when our internal message is right will they listen more readily to the external message we seek to share with them. Indeed, it is God's *plan* that the Church be the means by which His will for His people is accomplished.

This is God's way.

But is this Messianic Judaism's way?

If a Jewish person who is not yet a believer visited a Messianic synagogue, would he see God's way being presented? Would he be provoked to jealousy by what he saw?

God's Plan Affirmed

Almost as if he were anticipating my comments in this chapter, the Rev. Lloyd Elias Scalyer, a missionary in Pennsylvania, prepared and gave me a list of 23 quotes from noted Christian leaders affirming God's plan for the restoration of the Jewish people. I will share three of them with you:

Charles Haddon Spurgeon wrote this:

> I think we do not attach sufficient importance to the restoration of the Jews. We do not think enough of it. But certainly, if there is anything promised in the Bible, it is this. . . . The day shall yet come when the Jews, who were the first apostles to the Gentiles, the first missionaries to us, who were far off, shall be gathered in again. Until that shall be, the fullness of the Church's glory can never come. Matchless benefits to the world are bound up with the restoration of Israel. Their gathering in shall be as life from the dead.[1]

Jonathan Edwards wrote:

> Jewish infidelity shall be overthrown. . . . The Jews in all their dispersions shall cast away their old infidelity and shall have their hearts wonderfully changed, and abhor themselves for their past unbelief and obstinacy. They shall flow together to the blessed Jesus, penitently, humbly and joyfully owning Him as their glorious King and only Savior, and shall with all their hearts, as one heart and voice, declare His praises unto other nations. Nothing is more certainly foretold than this national conversion of the Jews in Romans 11. Besides the prophecies of the calling of the Jews, we have a remarkable providential seal of the fulfillment of this great event by a kind of continual miracle, viz. their being preserved a distinct nation. . . . The world affords nothing else like it. There is undoubtedly a remarkable hand of providence in it. When they shall be called, that ancient people, who alone were God's people for so long a time, shall be His people, never to be rejected more. They shall be gathered together into one fold, together with the Gentiles.[2]

Charles Hodge wrote:

The second great event, which, according to the common faith of the Church, is to precede the second advent of Christ, is the national conversion of the Jews. . . . That there is to be such a national conversion may be argued from the original call and destination of that people. . . . God did not deign to cast away His people entirely, but by their rejection, in the first place to facilitate the progress of the Gospel among the Gentiles, and ultimately to make the conversion of the Gentiles the means of converting the Jews. . . . The future restoration of the Jews is, in itself, a more probable event than the introduction of the Gentiles into the Church of God.[3]

These noted leaders back up what Scripture makes clear.

What About the Church?

At this point you could say, "Wait a minute. We need to take the log out of our own eye before we talk about the splinter in our brother's eye (see Matthew 7:5). Many in the Church also are not following God's way." Yes, I know. And that fact should cause all of us—those involved in Messianic Judaism, as well as those in the Church—to look again at the Word of God and then look into our mirrors. And we should repent and change our ways.

Consider the words of a friend of mine who is the Jewish pastor of a very nonrabbinic Messianic congregation:

I would suggest in a very humble manner that if the Church had done its job or if they had done fifty percent of their job, or if they had done 25 percent of their job, there would be no need for Messianic congregations, and they probably would not even exist as a movement. . . . Why should [a Jewish person] go into a congregation that does not pray for the peace of Jerusalem, that does not long to gather the Jewish people or even weep over them?

Yes, it is true. With some exceptions, the Church as a whole is not provoking the Jewish people to jealousy and is not bringing the Gospel to them. Indeed, the Church is not effectively doing its job.

But the question we are examining in this chapter is this: Is Messianic Judaism God's way? Is it doing the job? The answer should be very clear.

God's Will versus Tolerance

In considering the validity of Messianic Judaism, you might ask, "Wait a minute. Messianic Judaism is still a young movement. Shouldn't we just be more tolerant of it?"

A dictionary definition of the word *tolerance* reads, "sympathy or indulgence for beliefs or practices differing from or conflicting with one's own; the act of allowing something; the allowable deviation from a standard."[4] But the definition of the word *tolerance* in our society today is completely different from this.

Consider what is being taught to our children in public schools: "In order to be truly tolerant [according to the new tolerance], you must agree that another person's position is *just as valid as your own*." They say, "In order to be truly tolerant, you must give your approval, your endorsement, your sincere support *to their beliefs and behaviors*."

Josh McDowell and Bob Hostetler tell us, "The new tolerance may sound like the traditional tolerance but is vastly different. . . . This new tolerance is based on the unbiblical belief that 'truth is relative to the community in which a person participates. And since there are many human communities there are necessarily many different truths.'"[5]

Is this interpretation of the word *tolerance* correct? Are we required to approve of all lifestyles and actions of others even if they violate our conscience—even if they violate the Word of God? McDowell and Hostetler say no!

"The Bible makes it clear," they write, "that all values, beliefs, lifestyles and truth claims are not equal. It teaches that the God of the Bible is the true God (see Jeremiah 10:10), that all His words are true (see Psalm 119:160), and that if something is not right in God's sight, it is wrong (see Deuteronomy 6:18). This is not just the view of Hebrew culture or Christian culture or Western culture; it is the truth according to the God who rules over all cultures, revealed in God's Word."[6] Romans 12:2 clearly declares God's will:

> Do not be conformed to this world—this age, fashioned after and adapted to its external, superficial customs. But be transformed [changed] by the [entire] renewal of your mind—by its new ideals and its new attitude—so that you may prove [for yourselves] what is the good and acceptable and perfect will of God, even the thing which is good and acceptable and perfect [in His sight for you].
>
> AMP

Can I hear your Amen? Indeed, the current, popular philosophy of "tolerance" flies in the face of everything that we know about God and His Word.

No, we do not have to be more tolerant of Messianic Judaism. If we see that some of what it says and does contradicts God's way; if we see that its values, lifestyles and truth claims are contrary to what God says; if we see that it is dividing the Church; then we—especially Church leaders—*must* speak up.

> We must not support or encourage or sponsor or be "tolerant" of any activity that we know is inconsistent with God's Word.

We who are pastors, teachers or leaders in the Body of believers must consider for ourselves the truth of what has been presented and must firmly declare our observations to those who look to us for guidance. Silence in this matter could be confused with endorsement. We must not endorse what we know is inconsistent with God's will.

We must not support or encourage or sponsor *or be "tolerant" of* any activity that we know is inconsistent with God's Word. And this includes Messianic Judaism.

Fear of Being Labeled "Anti-Semitic"

And there is another question we should address: the question of anti-Semitism.

A number of years ago, when I was in the business world, I worked with many psychiatrists. I will never forget a statement that one well-known and highly respected psychiatrist made to me about the post-Holocaust attitude toward Jewish people. As clearly as I can remember, he said, "An interesting phenomenon has taken place in America: Following World War II there is a real reluctance to criticize anything that is 'Jewish.' The fear is that such criticism will label the person as anti-Semitic. And today, that is a most unpopular label for anyone to wear."

I sense a bit of this fear is present in some parts of the Church. There is a reluctance to criticize anything that appears to be "Jewish" for fear of the anti-Semitic label.

But just as we reject today's interpretation of the word *tolerant,* so we must reject this fear. If some of the teachings of Messianic Judaism are wrong, if they divide the Church and violate God's Word, we must say so. If we know that Messianic Judaism's purpose for being is flawed, we must say so.

My Position

Now let me be perfectly clear on this point: I am not implying that the beliefs and actions of our brothers and sisters in Messianic Judaism are wicked or that they intentionally violate God's Word. *I am not coming out against the individuals who are involved in Messianic Judaism.* Rather, I am speaking out against some of the things they are saying and some of the things they are doing because their way is not God's way. I have no doubt that the people involved in Messianic Judaism are most certainly good and well-meaning and sincerely want to serve the Lord. But I also have no doubt from what we have studied that they are involved with doctrines and actions that are inconsistent with His Word and that are contrary to His will for His Church—and His will for His chosen people.

In the next chapter, we will look at what the Church needs to do in order to remedy its past mistakes and begin to reach out and "provoke Israel to jealousy."

11

WHAT DOES THE CHURCH NEED TO DO?

Now that we have taken a look at God's will and plan for His Church, do I hear you asking, "Where do *I* fit into God's plan?"

We must first understand that God does not want His Church to be passive about His will or about His plan to reach the Jewish people. He wants us to be actively involved in reaching out to the Jewish people—indeed to all people—with His love. He wants us to proclaim His Gospel to all who have ears to hear—and eyes to see—from Jerusalem to Judea, to Samaria and to the uttermost parts of the world. He does not want any to perish but all to receive eternal life (see 2 Peter 3:9). And that word *any* includes the Jewish people!

If a church wants to do God's will, it must make praying for and reaching out to Jewish people—as well as *all* others—a positive part of its purpose for being. It *must* reach out with the wonderful good news of the Gospel.

First Understand "Why"

From time to time, I am asked to suggest ways for believers to reach their Jewish friends. Almost always, I answer that question by saying, "Before we can discuss *how*, we must discuss *why*." Then I ask the person to pretend that he or she is Jewish and to read all of Deuteronomy 28. I encourage you to do the same, right now.

In the first fourteen verses of this chapter, you will find the blessings that await Jewish people if we keep *all* of God's 613 commandments. And those blessings are wonderful.

> If a church wants to do God's will, it must make praying for and reaching out to Jewish people—as well as all others—a positive part of its purpose for being.

But beginning with verse 15 and for the next 53 verses you will find the terrible curses that will be upon our heads and the heads of our children if we do not keep *all* of God's 613 commandments. Often I sit quietly by while a person reads this entire chapter, and I watch his facial expressions change as he reads the 53 verses of cursing in this chapter. Those curses are horrible in and of themselves. But the greatest curse of all is eternal separation from God. It is only by repenting of our sin and coming into God's new covenant of grace by faith that we can be redeemed from these curses and restored to God.

It is my hope and prayer that your heart, as well as your mind, will comprehend the enormity of the truths you have just read. It is also my hope that if you know any Jewish people, if you care about any Jewish people, if you love any Jewish people, you will want to bring to them the Gospel of peace. Surely you now realize that the most anti-Semitic thing you can do is to withhold the Gospel from them. And if you know that, you are ready to be used by God.

Very well, you understand "why." Now you are ready to consider "how."

First Things First: What Do They Believe?

One of the most important first steps you can take is to understand what category your Jewish friends are in. Which of the following things do they say about what they believe?

1. I do not believe in God.
2. I believe in God but see the Bible only as the story of the Jewish people.
3. I do not really know if I believe in God or the Bible, but I believe that personal "religion" is important.
4. I understand little of contemporary Judaism, but I feel an obligation to maintain my Jewish identity through observance of customs and traditions.
5. I hold an antisupernatural view of Scripture. I appreciate its ethical values but do not view the Bible as a book from God that is binding upon my life.
6. I am antireligious. I do not define myself by my Jewishness.
7. I value my Jewish heritage and have accepted its morals and cultural values, but I am not involved in a synagogue.
8. I am confused.

It has been my experience that most Jewish people are in this last category. But no matter which of the eight categories your Jewish friends say they are in, one thing is certain: They have been conditioned to believe that Jesus is *not* their Messiah.

Overcoming Some Myths

Before we go any further, I want to help you overcome three myths that may have caused you concern in the past.

Myth Number 1: Jewish people know the Hebrew Scriptures better than you do. As I have pointed out, this is not true in 99.9 percent of the cases.

Myth Number 2: You must approach Jewish people within the context of Judaism. As I have also previously explained, less than seven percent of American Jews attend a synagogue on a regular basis. Most are not seriously involved with "Judaism."

Myth Number 3: It is best if a Jewish person reaches out to other Jewish people. This, too, is false. The overwhelming majority of Jewish believers were reached by their Gentile friends.

Reaching the Jewish People on an Individual Basis

After overcoming these myths and learning what your Jewish friends believe, I encourage you not to be afraid to reach out to them with God's love. Appreciate them as individuals. Appreciate their Jewishness—whatever that means to them.

Always remember that God's way is the way of love and that God wants you to provoke your Jewish friends to jealousy. "Friendship evangelism" is important, especially with your Jewish friends, but you must never forget the "evangelism" part of that phrase.

Pray for an opportunity to have a spiritual conversation with them. Share your testimony. Ask them questions and *listen* to their answers. Then let them ask you questions. Ask, "Who do you say that Jesus is?" And point out who *you* say that Jesus is and *why* you say so—from Scripture.

In chapter 8 you read the statistics that reveal that most Jewish believers were initially attracted to Jesus by what they saw in the lives of their believing friends and relatives. But the most important factor in their decision to accept Jesus as Lord of their lives was the Gospel itself. The Gospel is, after all, God's power (see Romans 1:16) and we should rely on it.

How the Local Church Can Reach Jews

When I was pastoring, people often would ask me to describe the makeup of our church. Usually I would respond, "It is as if God used a huge crane with a tremendous scoop and dropped the scoop on our community. Then after it picked up lots and lots of people, He raised the scoop, moved it to our facility and lowered it, gently placing the people into our church."

Since we were located in Maryland, just outside of Washington, D.C., people of every color and background attended our church. By the third year of our congregation's life, we had more than 30 Jewish people, 110 former Catholics and 150 Protestants from many different denominations. We hardly ever discussed the things that used to divide us as we concentrated on the One who unites us. Truly it was a loving and caring church that was hungry to learn God's Word and to do His will.

139

We had a large percentage of African-Americans in our congregation because our neighborhood had a large percentage of African-Americans. But we also had many Asians, Hispanics, American Indians and Jewish members because they lived in our neighborhood, too. The point I want you to see is that every ethnic group was welcome, but we never stressed ethnicity as the *basis* of our relationship. Because I am Jewish, our church had a Jewish flavor. How could it not? But Jesus said, "But I, when I am lifted up from the earth, will draw all men to myself" (John 12:32), and almost every week we saw that truth come alive within our congregation.

What about your church? Are you reaching out to the nonbelievers in your community? What about the Jewish people?

Of course, it may be that there are almost no Jewish people in your community and that if God lowered His scoop, He might pick up more and more people just like you. You may not have any Jewish neighbors. You may not even know any Jewish people. That's okay. But you can still pray for the peace of Jerusalem and for the Jews to come to the Messiah. And you can pray that God will send laborers to us.

But what if your church is in a community where there *are* many Jewish people? What might you do to attract them? I will never forget Pastor MacArthur Jollay of the Christ Church of Washington in Washington, D.C. He often led us to pray for the peace of Jerusalem. He frequently shared with us his love and God's love for the Jewish people. Every few years, he would lead a tour to Israel. He often preached from the Hebrew Scriptures and showed how the feasts of Israel were fulfilled in Jesus. He *wanted* to have Jewish people in his congregation. And they came.

I have been told that one church in Los Angeles had more than five hundred Jewish members. I suspect that the pastor of that church understands God's heart for the Jewish people just as Pastor Jollay did.

But do you have to dress up in synagogue attire, take down the cross and have lots and lots of Messianic music in your church in order to attract Jewish people? No. But since I mentioned it, Messianic music is wonderful, and it certainly would make those Jewish people who do attend your church quite comfortable. It would let them know that you appreciate their Jewishness and are aware of how important Messianic music can be to voicing that appreciation. And Gentile believers enjoy Messianic music, too.

What about holding Passover Seders every year, or every few years? Great idea. These are wonderful times to remind your congregation how Jesus celebrated the Last Supper. And these also are great opportunities to pray for and reach out to the Jewish people in your community.

For many years, I have been presenting "Christ in the Passover" in many different denominational churches, and no matter the denomination, the congregation's response is always the same. The people love it. The Jewish friends they invite to the service love it. But note: In these instances the Seder is not exhibited as a matter of religious duty. Jewish history and culture—not rabbinic Judaism—are being presented. And wonderful opportunities to share the Gospel are created when the Passover is communicated in this way.

What about other Jewish holidays? Do churches *have to* observe them? Of course not. But again, they represent wonderful opportunities to help the people understand the faithfulness of God and to see how Jesus fulfilled each of these holidays.

What about inviting Jewish ministers to speak at your church? Another great idea! But make certain that the ministers you choose proclaim first and foremost the

141

Lordship of Jesus. Only secondarily should they share insight about Jewish life and views, which carry no spiritual authority.

What about continually reminding your church how important it is to pray for and reach out to their Jewish friends? Yes.

What about teaching about the Jewish roots of the Church? The people will be blessed.

What about reminding your church to support Jewish ministries? Of course.

I am certain that as you more fully appreciate God's heart for the Jewish people and His will that you share the Gospel with them, you will find many other ways to express His will in your life and the life of your congregation. But let prayer undergird all of your efforts. Pray for the peace of Jerusalem, as God directs us to do (see Psalm 122:6). Pray for wisdom. Pray for God's anointing. Pray that a mustard seed of faith will arise in the heart of every Jewish person for whom you pray.

But most of all, remember that God wants you to be actively involved in His will and His plan to reach the Jewish people. He wants you to show them His love and to proclaim His Gospel to His chosen—and to all—people.

What a privilege it is to be used by God in this way!

12

BEWARE THE DIVIDED HEART

To introduce the subject of the dangers of a divided heart, I will tell you a quick story. A number of years ago, with the pastor of a Baptist church, I cohosted a popular talk show on a Christian radio station in the Washington, D.C., area. The program was so successful that it attracted the attention of a national advertising agency specializing in Christian radio. They approached us, and we held a series of meetings to consider if we could successfully break into the national Christian radio market. They told us that if we could, we would be able to accomplish many things for the Lord and earn a great deal of money for ourselves.

During one of our early sessions, the agency representative suggested that we expand our number to three pastors. That way each of us could specialize in a different area of ministry, adding a great deal of variety to the broadcast and making the program more interesting. We accepted his suggestion. When the three of us met with the agency rep, he recommended that we put together a mission statement. He encouraged us to spend as much time as needed to put that statement together. Then he said, "Each of you must agree on every word in your mission statement. Until you are in total agreement, our agency will not be able to do anything for you."

He also told us that after we got the program started, every person who would ever work in this ministry would have to agree totally with our mission statement. And if the time came when they did not agree, they were to be fired immediately. No divided hearts were to be allowed in this ministry.

Clearly the agency was interested in the financial, as well as the spiritual, success of this new radio ministry and was concerned that if any of us took our eyes off the mission, division would arise within us and the ministry would be weakened. Without going into detail, let me just say that in less than a year, for reasons that none of us had even considered, a division did come up between us and our hearts became divided. Not much later, the program went off the air.

I often wondered if the story of the Tower of Babel in Genesis 11 was the spiritual basis for the ad agency's position. You may remember the story. When the people in Babel were all saying the same thing and envisioning the same goal, God said:

> Behold, they are one people, and they have all one language; and this is only the beginning of what they will do; and now nothing they have imagined they can do will be impossible to them. Come, let Us go down, and there confound [mix up, confuse] their language, that they may not understand one another's speech. So the Lord

scattered them abroad from that place upon the face of the whole earth; and they gave up building the city.

Genesis 11:6–8, AMP

Was that the motivation behind the advertising agency's recommendations? It could well have been. In business it is imperative that the core mission of the business be the focus of everyone working in that business, and this is even truer for those in ministry.

A Lesson from Hosea

Years later I learned another important spiritual lesson that could have applied to our radio program and focuses on the subject of a divided heart. Let me share it with you.

You may remember that the prophet Hosea prophesied to the northern kingdom of Israel at about the same time that Isaiah prophesied to the southern kingdom of Judah. At that time idolatry and evil were the hallmarks of the northern kingdom. During the reign of King Ahab, perhaps the most wicked of all the kings of Israel, the people worshipped Baal and golden calves and many other idols. And four of the six kings before Ahab had been murdered and then succeeded by the ones who murdered them. It was into this evil setting that God sent Hosea to speak forth His Word and to draw the people back to God.

In order to fully appreciate the irony of what Hosea was about to do, you need to gain some insight into his life. In the first chapter of this book, we learn that God instructed Hosea to marry Gomer. At best, Gomer was an adulteress. At worst, she was a prostitute. God had instructed Hosea to love and have children with Gomer. But before and even after the children came, Gomer took other lovers and had many affairs. Hosea forgave her after each one. When she came back to him, Gomer probably appeared to repent and confess her love for Hosea. She might have even vowed to be faithful. But then the temptation would rise within her and she would go back to her sin. Yet after each of her adventures, Hosea took Gomer back.

The lesson we see in Hosea's life with Gomer is a picture of God's attitude toward the people of Israel. He loves us but hates our sins. And so, in spite of everything we have done, He promises to forgive us and bless us again if we will return to Him and be faithful to Him.

Hosea tells us of the dangers of a divided heart. Gomer is an example of that: She had a little bit of love for God and a little bit of love for Hosea and a little bit of love for her children and more than a little bit of love for her lovers. She loved none of them fully.

You cannot serve the Lord fully if you have a divided heart!

The strong lesson in this story applies to Messianic Judaism as well as the Church as a whole. Here is the point you must see: You cannot serve the Lord fully if you have a divided heart! You cannot love God a little bit and also love the world a little bit. The world system contains so many temptations. The TV screens scream at us. The magazines add their screams. And for our purposes, let us also recognize that the Jewish community adds its screams. And the rabbis add theirs. And Jewishness adds its. And our hearts become divided. We lose our focus. We want Jesus, but we also want A, B, C and D. And sometimes we appear to want A, B, C and D more than we want Jesus. Certainly some of us spend more of our time and energy thinking and talking about these "idols" than we do thinking and talking about the Lord.

We need to resolve to have a whole heart, a heart

BEWARE THE DIVIDED HEART

that is wholly focused on the Lord and His Word. Why? Because there is tremendous danger in having a divided heart.

Some time ago I heard a message by Pastor Scott Young at the Church of Hope in Sarasota, Florida. He was teaching about Hosea and listed three things that happen when a person or a church has a divided heart. First, a divided heart corrupts the truth. Second, a divided heart makes its own god. And third, a divided heart breeds conflict.[1]

Consider what Hosea said in chapter 10, verse 2: "Their heart is deceitful, and now they must bear their guilt. The LORD will demolish their altars and destroy their sacred stones." The English word *deceitful* comes from the root word for ancient Hebraic "lots" that were cast in order to divide things. When Jesus died on the cross, they cast lots in order to divide His belongings. The same root word was used. So you could read this verse as saying, "Their heart is divided, and now they must bear their guilt."

> *We want Jesus, but we also want A, B, C and D. And sometimes we appear to want A, B, C and D more than we want Jesus.*

How This Applies to Messianic Judaism

Now watch the application to Messianic Judaism. It seems to have a little bit of God and a little bit of Torah service, a little bit of Hebrew, a little bit of bread and wine, a little bit of yarmulke wearing, a little bit of keeping kosher, and lots of Messianic music and Israeli folk dancing. And before you know it, these things are spoken of more than we speak of Yeshua. The heart has been divided, and the truth has been corrupted.

147

Then we see the new religion being formed. We are being conformed to Jewish practices rather than being transformed into the image of the Lord Jesus.

And think about the truth that a divided heart makes up its own god (see Hosea 10:2). When we feel that we cannot reach the standard God has set, we make the decision to lower the standard. And in effect we are making up our own rules and our own god. Hosea 10:13 speaks of this: "But you have planted wickedness, you have reaped evil, you have eaten the fruit of deception. Because you have depended on your own strength and on your many warriors."

What does this verse say to us today? It tells us that our efforts to please the Jewish community by extolling Jewishness lowers God's standard and gives us a new god to worship. Jesus said, "If I be lifted up, I will draw all men unto me" (see John 12:32). But by lifting up rabbinic form and synagogue life and the emphasis on pleasing the Jewish community, hasn't Messianic Judaism become a different religion, and aren't those who embrace it worshiping a false god?

We have to hold God's standard high. We cannot compromise God's Word. We are not to have a little bit of God and a little bit of this and a little bit of that. When you see that happening in your life, you have to know that you have allowed your heart to be divided. You are relying on your own strength, your own warriors, your own definitions and your own idols, and you are veering from God and His Word.

And certainly you can understand that a divided heart creates conflict. In Hosea 10:4 we read, "They make many promises, take false oaths and make agreements; therefore lawsuits spring up like poisonous weeds in a plowed field."

A divided heart lies very easily. Disagreements and confrontations abound. The people are not honest, loving and gracious toward one another. They wink and nod and rationalize with one another, keeping their own counsel and not living their lives in accordance with God's Word. Unforgiveness, jealousy, resentment and hostility raise their ugly heads. How, then, can those with divided hearts walk together to proclaim God's love?

A Strong Word of Correction

Messianic Judaism's divided heart and emphasis on following rabbinic form can subtly detract from the clear teaching of God's Word:

> It is by free grace (God's unmerited favor) that you are saved (delivered from judgment and made partakers of Christ's salvation) through [your] faith. And this [salvation] is not of yourselves—of your own doing, it came not through your own striving—but it is the gift of God; Not because of works [not the fulfillment of the Law's demands], lest any man should boast. [It is not the result of what any one can possibly do, so no one can pride himself in it or take glory to himself.] For we are God's [own] handiwork (His workmanship), recreated in Christ Jesus, [born anew] that we may do those good works which God predestined (planned beforehand) for us.
>
> Ephesians 2:8–10, AMP

> O you poor and silly and thoughtless and unreflecting and senseless Galatians! Who has fascinated or bewitched or cast a spell over you, unto whom—right before your very eyes—Jesus Christ, the Messiah, was openly and graphically set forth and portrayed as crucified?
>
> Let me ask you this one question: Did you receive the (Holy) Spirit as the result of obeying the Law and doing its works, or was it by hearing [the message of

the Gospel] and believing [it]?—Was it from observing
a law of rituals or from a message of faith?

Galatians 3:1–2, AMP

I know that almost all leaders in Messianic Judaism
would insist that salvation is solely by faith through
God's grace. But the actions and attitudes of their (primarily Gentile) followers seem to indicate a belief that
if Jewish people are *really* saved, they should belong to
Messianic synagogues and follow rabbinic form.

Somehow in the midst of my brothers' emphasis on
Messianic Judaism, they have lost sight of two facts
that we already have discussed: (1) God has not called
us to an ethnic identity, and (2) He has clearly called
us—Jews and Gentiles alike—to spiritual identity as
one new man.

Seeking an Undivided Heart

How do we solve this problem? When the flow of
blood in a human heart is blocked, a bypass must be
performed. In the same way, when our spiritual hearts
are divided and the flow of God's love is blocked, we
need a spiritual bypass. But we cannot look to someone
else to perform the surgery. Each of us has to perform it
for him- or herself. We must see how far we have fallen
from the path God set forth, repent and turn back to
God with an undivided heart.

Think about what Moses taught in Deuteronomy
6:4–5. We love to chant these verses in Hebrew. After
all, we are declaring the *Sh'ma*, the watchword of our
faith. And when together we chant these words in Hebrew, it seems to be something mystical. Somehow we
even feel closer to God. But have we really thought about
the meaning of the words we chant?

150

"Hear, O Israel: the LORD our God is one LORD; And you shall love the LORD your God with all your heart and with all your soul and with all your might." The key word in this verse is *all*.

Each and every believer is to love the Lord with ALL his heart.

He is to love the Lord with ALL his soul.

He is to love the Lord with ALL his mind and strength.

God's plan has no room for a divided heart. It cannot be Jesus and a little bit of this and a little bit of that. No portion of one's heart is to be compartmentalized. We are to love the Lord with ALL our hearts.

> *God's plan has no room for a divided heart.*

Let there be no doubt about what God wants in our relationship with Him. He wants us to recognize that He is the Alpha and the Omega, the beginning and the end. And we are to worship no other gods before Him. Our might and our abilities and our traditions and our practices are meaningless before Him. Hasn't He told us that He is tired of our sacrifices and oblations? He wants us to come to Him with clean lips, clean hands and an undivided heart.

The first-century Christians were on fire with the reality of the resurrection of Jesus from the dead! They were in agreement, and the power of an undivided heart was loosed through them. To every Jewish person who had ears to hear, they proclaimed: *Jesus is our Messiah. In order to restore us to God, He took our sins upon Himself and was crushed in our place. Isaiah's prophecy has been fulfilled! And God raised Jesus from the dead so that we would understand! Because of what Jesus did, you can be saved from the wrath of God and be reconciled to Him. You need to repent of your sins and by faith confess Him as your Lord!* And the Church grew daily. More and

151

more Jewish people received Him as Messiah and Lord of their lives. Then they proclaimed the Good News to the Gentiles. And the world was changed.

The Bible teaches us that one day Jewish evangelists will be loosed on the world. Their hearts will not be divided. They will obey God's Word fully. They will say the same thing. They will do the same thing. They will accomplish the same thing. They will be God's representatives, His ambassadors, His witnesses to a lost and dying world. And the power of their agreement will make it possible for them to do everything they can imagine themselves doing.

But why do we have to wait until that day? Why can't we Jewish believers start doing what God wants us to do right now? Did I hear you say, "Even the Church is not doing that?" That's right. The hearts of many in the Church also are divided. Satan, too, knows the power of agreement. And if he can keep us divided, he will keep us from doing God's will. But again I say that God wants us to be in agreement with Him!

Awesome Power

Picture with me what would happen if we forgot about our "denominational chariots" and our "end-time warriors" and our "different positions" and began to let our living God be the focus of our lives and ministry. Can you see it? When each of us who has proclaimed Jesus as Lord of our lives makes the decision to be exactly who God said we are to be—one new man—and to do exactly what God said we are to do—proclaim the Gospel to all who have ears to hear—then the power that will be unleashed will be awesome. None will be able to resist it.

And Israel *will* be provoked to jealousy rather than rage! And all Israel will be saved.

Is that an impossible dream? Am I talking about what it will be like in heaven? No, I am not. I believe that what I have described is precisely what God wants to see happening among Jewish believers, among Gentile believers, among tall people, short people and people of every color, size and shape and in every land.

In John 17, Jesus prayed that we would be one as He and the Father are One. Why are we not one? Because we have allowed our hearts to be divided. As we have concentrated on our own strength and our own opinions and our own beliefs, we have veered further and further away from God's Word and His will for us as we live our lives on earth.

> **Why are we not one? Because we have allowed our hearts to be divided.**

The Results of a Divided Heart

I remember a meeting that was held in 1981 in a log cabin in remote Maryland outside of Washington, D.C. I called an "Acts 15 in Reverse" meeting of a number of ministers who were either in the movement or were concerned about it. And the question I posed to the group was this: "What must Jewish people who accept Jesus as Messiah and Lord do after they believe?"

Five ministers were present at the meeting. Two were Gentile pastors. I was the Jewish pastor, and there was one Jewish evangelist who was very actively involved in Messianic Judaism. The fifth man was an assistant pastor in a local church whose mother was Jewish but who had not been raised in Judaism.

For an entire day we sat around a table in the living room of a log cabin. No phones. No distractions. We prayed together at length, and then we discussed the pluses and minuses of Messianic Judaism.

We talked about the direction the movement was headed. We talked about the possible elitism, pride and separatism that were coming into the movement. We talked about the emphasis on works rather than God's grace. We talked about the division the movement might cause in the Body of Christ. We talked about the need for the Church to be more sensitive to the needs of Jewish believers. And we talked about how serious an error it was to place the emphasis of the movement on rabbinic Judaism instead of Jewish culture. There was much agreement and some disagreement among us as we considered these issues. As the day was ending, the Jewish evangelist who was with us said this: "Maybe we should not have used the words *Messianic Judaism*. But we did, and it is too late now to change it. Messianic Judaism *is!*"

It was on that note that our "Acts 15 in Reverse" meeting ended.

More than 25 years have passed since I first recognized the potential problems of Messianic Judaism. During this time I have waited for the movement to become more stable and for the needed corrections to be made. But they have not been made. Instead, with the passing years, the problems have increased and intensified.

Further, as we reflect on how few Jewish people Messianic Judaism has attracted and how many Jewish people it has antagonized and offended, we can see that it has not accomplished one of the major purposes it has declared for its existence.

A Challenge to Messianic Judaism

But it is not too late. Accordingly I now address my brothers and sisters who are involved in Messianic Judaism. I exhort you to:

154

1. Recognize the tremendous difference that exists between Jewish culture and rabbinic form. I urge you to end your emphasis on rabbinic form.
2. Recognize that while Messianic congregations can be a bridge between the synagogue and the Church, no one builds a home on a bridge.
3. Recognize that it is God's will that together we be one new man. There is to be *one* Church.

Will the leaders in the movement accept this challenge? I am not sure. Will they understand that if God does not have ALL of your heart, then He does not have you? I am not sure.

In May 2003 I helped form the International Jewish Evangelical Fellowship. At the conclusion of our very first meeting, we prayed and then called upon our fellow Jewish believers and the Church to carefully read and respond to the following statements:

> We gathered because we love God and believe the message of salvation He has sent "for Jews first and also for Gentiles" (see Acts 3:26; Romans 1:16).

> We call upon our people to turn from the errors of secularism and rabbinicism, to repent and to put their trust in Jesus, Israel's promised Messiah (see Acts 3:19–26). Rabbinic Judaism was created in the course of our people's exiles and represents a departure from the biblical faith of Israel.

> We call upon our Jewish brethren in the faith who are in evangelical churches around the world to be faithful in their respective churches and not to succumb to the demand to gather in ethnically focused congregations. We believe that none but God in Messiah should be the focus of individual and congregation life (see Colossians 1:18).

We call upon our Jewish brethren in the faith who are in evangelical churches to make their distinct contribution to the Church.

We call upon our Jewish brethren in the faith to retain, cultivate and nourish their Jewish identity (see 1 Corinthians 7:17–18) as a matter of national and cultural heritage, not as an aspect of their obedience to God (see Romans 2:25; Galatians 5:6; 6:15). God never commanded us to be Jewish. But He called upon us to love Him sincerely, to strive for godliness and high moral standards, and to honestly care for our fellow man.

We call upon the evangelical Church to accommodate itself more fully to accept and respect the Jewish Christians in its midst and to rid itself of thought patterns and expressions that have anti-Semitic roots. Jews who cherish their national and cultural identity are not necessarily Judaizing (see Romans 11:1).

We call upon the evangelical Church to renew its recognition of the Bible, not rabbinic Judaism, as the roots of its faith. Rabbinic Judaism ought to be challenged, not embraced.

We call upon the evangelical Church to renew its commitment to "provoke Israel to jealousy" (see Romans 11:11) by its holiness and godly conduct and to proclaim the Good News of the Messiah to the Jewish people.

We call upon our Jewish brethren in the faith who gather in their separate congregations to renew their commitment to the truth and supreme authority of Scripture, and to reaffirm

• that the Father, Son and Spirit are fully equal in Their deity;
• that the Mosaic Covenant was "our schoolmaster to lead us to Messiah." Now that He has come we are

"no longer under the schoolmaster" (see Galatians 3:24–25);

- that being Jewish or maintaining Jewish custom in no way promotes spirituality, holiness or proximity to God;
- that the Body of Christ is one in which Jews and Gentiles, members of all and any race, are united—as are men and women or people from various social, educational, financial or political strata.

We call upon informed adherents to Messianic Judaism to dialogue with us: We love and respect you. We humbly differ with you on important issues. We are eager to hear and be heard, so that you and we might together better serve God and Messiah's cause.

It is my heartfelt prayer that *you* will agree with each of these statements.

I pray, too, that you will express your oneness in Messiah Jesus with your Jewish and Gentile believing brothers and sisters. As you do so, the power of agreement will be loosed in your life and you will activate the ministry God has given you—even more.

In Acts 15:19, the Spirit of God speaking through James said, "It is my opinion that we should not put obstacles in the way and annoy and disturb those of the Gentiles who turn to God" (AMP).

Today I believe the Spirit of God is saying, *It is My will that we not put obstacles in the way of the Jewish people who are turning to God.*

A Greater Purpose

I end now with this thought: God has been keeping the Jewish people as a separate people down through the centuries. Why? Because our coming to repentance and faith in the last days will give us, as a people, the unique task of carrying to completion the worldwide eschatological task of proclaiming to the nations the final witness to the Gospel.

Most assuredly Satan wants to keep this from happening. That is why he is increasing his efforts to keep the Gospel from the Jewish people—to divide us and to destroy us. We Jewish and Gentile believers in Jesus must not allow ourselves to be used by him to keep God's will from being done.

Will you join me in saying *Amen*?

EPILOGUE

If there is one statement that can be made about the condition of the Church throughout the world today, it is this: We have allowed our hearts to be divided, and our concerns about what "we believe" have separated us from other disciples of the Lord Jesus—and have weakened the Church.

When I set out to write this book, my primary purpose was to address Messianic Judaism. Secondarily, I wanted to speak to those in the Church who have concerns about this movement.

I now believe that God's message has much wider application. Many of us have allowed our churches, our denominations and our movements to become institutionalized. For many, methodology has become our purpose. I say again, *we have allowed our hearts to be divided and our concerns about what "we believe" have separated us from—and weakened—the Church.*

> *For many, methodology has become our purpose.*

God has not called us to focus on our churches, our denominations or our movements. They are not to become our purpose. Every "Union," every "Alliance," every "–ism," every "–ic" and every thought of "our way or the highway" must be laid aside as we recommit ourselves to being the people—the *kainos*—that Jesus said we are to be so that we can do what He said we are to do.

Each one of us must realize that we will only be able to do so if we rise above the things that divide us and once again focus in obedience on the One who unites us. It is *His* will that is to be done.

As one new man we are to go to the uttermost parts of the world *in unity* as we proclaim the wonderful truth of the Gospel. Let the words of Jesus to God the Father on our behalf be heard again:

> Sanctify them by the truth; your word is truth. As you sent me into the world, I have sent them into the world. For them I sanctify myself, that they too may be truly sanctified.
>
> My prayer is not for them alone, I pray also for those who will believe in me through their message, that all of them may be one, Father, just as you are in me and I am in you. May they also be in us so that the world may believe that you have sent me.
>
> John 17:17–21

And may His words to the Church mobilize us to action:

> All authority in heaven and on earth has been given to me. Therefore go and make disciples of all nations, baptizing them in the name of the Father and of the Son and of the Holy Spirit, and teaching them to obey everything I have commanded you.
>
> Matthew 28:18–20

You and I must search our hearts today and ask ourselves if we have strayed from doing God's will. Are our hearts divided? Are we more concerned about obeying the rules of our denomination than we are about obeying God's Word? Are we more concerned about our ethnic identity than we are about the new identity God has given us? Are we provoking Israel to jealousy? Are we proclaiming God's Word? Are we making disciples? Are we doing what God has commanded us to do?

Are we?

If not, we must repent and recommit ourselves to obeying our Lord.

I pray that the power of agreement with God will be loosed in you . . . and in me . . . and throughout the Body of Christ as we wait for Him to come again.

Maranatha. Amen.

NOTES

Introduction

1. David H. Stern, "Summary Essay: The Future of Messianic Judaism," *How Jewish Is Christianity? Two Views on the Messianic Movement*, Stanley N. Gundrey, series ed., Louis Goldberg, general ed. (Grand Rapids: Zondervan, 2003), 178–79.

Chapter 1

1. William Varner, "Messianic Congregations Are Not Necessary," *How Jewish Is Christianity?* 48.

Chapter 2

1. See also Deuteronomy 12:32; Joshua 1:7; Hosea 9–11; Jeremiah 3:6–18 and 16:10–13; Lamentations 1–4.

2. Paul Johnson, *History of the Jews* (New York: Harper and Row, 1987), 165.

3. Malcolm Hay, *The Roots of Christian Anti-Semitism* (New York: Liberty Press, 1981), 27.

4. Information retreieved from website: http://www.fordham.edu/halsall/source/chrysostom-jews6.html#HOMILY_I.

5. Information retrieved from website: http://www.aish.com/literacy/jewishhistory/Crash_Course_in_Jewish_History_Part_45_-_The_Crusades.asp.

6. Abram Leon Sachar, *A History of the Jews* (New York: Alfred Knopf, 1965), 191–92.

7. Ibid.

8. Chaim Potok, *Wanderings* (New York: Fawcett Crest Books, 1978), 423.

9. Cecil Roth, *A History of the Marranos* (New York: Shocken, 1974), 32.

10. Ktav/Anti-Defamation League of B'nai B'rith, 1975, 33.

11. Information retrieved from website: http://www.fordham.edu/ halsall/source/chrysostom- jews6.html#HOMILY_I.

12. Johnson, *History*, 242.

13. Max I. Dimont, *Jews, God and History* (New York: Simon and Schuster, 1961), 234.

14. Raul Hilberg, *The Destruction of the European Jews* (New York: Holmes & Meier, 1985), 8–9.

Chapter 4

1. Baruch Maoz, *Judaism Is Not Jewish* (Ross-shire, Great Britain: Christian Focus Publications, 2003), 319.

2. Ibid, 320.

3. Ibid.

4. Kai Kjaer-Hansen, International Coordinator of the Lausanne Consultation on Jewish Evangelism, *LCJE Bulletin*, May 2003, 4–10.

5. Maoz, *Judaism*, 321.

6. Ibid.

7. Ibid, 324.

8. Ibid, 325.

Chapter 5

1. From the website of the Union of Messianic Jewish Congregations, http://www.umjc.org/aboutmj/whatismj.htm. Provided by Congregation Roeh Israel of Denver, Colorado. Updated February 28, 2003.

2. Ibid.

3. Michael L. Brown, Ph.D., "Tradition or Truth? What I Learned about Rabbinic Judaism," *They Thought for Themselves* by Sid Roth (Brunswick, Ga.: MV Press, 1999), 132.

4. Michael L. Brown, Ph.D., "The Place of Rabbinic Tradition in Messianic Judaism," at the following website: http://www.icnministries.org/articles/rabtrad/rabtrad.doc.
5. Union of Messianic Jewish Congregations website.
6. Ibid
7. Ibid.
8. Ibid.
9. Gundrey and Goldberg, *How Jewish?* 68.
10. Maoz, *Judaism*, 236.

Chapter 8

1. David Sedaca, Executive Secretary of the International Messianic Jewish Alliance, "Outreach through Messianic Congregations—A History and Insight for Today," Bulletin of the Lausanne Consultation on Jewish Evangelism, May 2003, p.13.
2. Ibid, 13–14.
3. Abigail Radoszkowicz, in an article (title unknown) of *The Jerusalem Post*, June 7, 2003. In this article the author quotes Jamie Cowan, head of the UMJC (Union of Messianic Jewish Congregations).
4. Gundrey and Goldberg, *How Jewish?* 185.
5. Sedaca, 14.
6. Gundrey and Goldberg, *How Jewish?* 68.
7. Stan Telchin, *Abandoned* (Grand Rapids: Chosen Books, 1997), 192–93.

Chapter 9

1. Lisa Loden in a paper delivered in August 2003 at the World Conference of the Lausanne Consultation on Jewish Evangelism in Helsinki, Finland.
2. Arthur Goldberg in a paper delivered in August 2003 at the World Conference of the LCJE in Helsinki, Finland.
3. Loden.
4. Kai Kjaer-Hansen and Bodil F. Skjøtt, *Facts and Myths about the Messianic Congregations in Israel* (Jerusalem: Caspari Center, 1999).
5. Statement by Kai Kjaer-Hansen at the Seventh North American Coordinating Committee of the LCJE held in Atlanta March 13–15, 2000.
6. Maoz, *Judaism*, 49.
7. Ibid.

Chapter 10

1. Charles Spurgeon, *Spurgeon's Sermons*, vol. 17 (Grand Rapids: Christian Classics Etherial Library, 1871), 703–4.
2. Jonathan, Edwards, *The Works of Jonathan Edwards*, vol. 1 (Edinburgh, U.K.: Banner of Truth Trust, 1976), 607.
3. Charles Hodge, *Systematic Theology*, vol. 3 (Edinburgh, U.K.: James Clark & Co., 1906), 805.
4. *Webster's Seventh New Collegiate Dictionary* (Springfield: G and C Merriam Company, 1965), 930.
5. Josh D. McDowell and Bob Hostetler, *The New Tolerance* (Wheaton: Tyndale House, 1999), 18.
6. Ibid, 23.

Chapter 12

1. I am indebted to Pastor Scott for the clarity of his observations. From them, many of my own observations have been developed.

FOR FURTHER READING

Danielou, Jean. *The Theology of Jewish Christianity: A History of Early Christian Doctrine Before the Council of Nicaea, Vol. 1*, London: Darton Longman and Todd Ltd.; and Pennsylvania: Westminster Press, 1964.

Feher, Shoshana. *Passing Over Easter: Constructing the Boundaries of Messianic Judaism.* Walnut Creek: Alta Mira Press, 1998.

Fruchtenbaum, Arnold G. *Hebrew Christianity: Its Theology, History and Philosophy.* Washington, D.C.: Canon, 1974.

Goldberg, Arthur. "Main Obstacles and My Joy." LCJE Bulletin. Arthus, Denmark, August 10, 2003.

Gundrey, Stanley N. and Louis Goldberg. "How Jewish Is Christianity?" Grand Rapids: Zondervan, 2003.

Hay, Malcolm. *The Roots of Christian Anti-Semitism.* New York: Liberty Press, 1981.

Hilberg, Raul. *The Destruction of the European Jews.* New York: Holmes & Meier, 1985.

Hort, Fenton John Anthony. *Judaistic Christianity.* Grand Rapids: Baker, 1980.

Jocz, Jakob. *The Jewish People and Jesus Christ: A Study in the Controversy between Church and Synagogue.* S.P.C.K, 1979.

Johnson, Paul. *History of the Jews.* New York: Harper and Row, 1987.

Juster, Daniel. *Jewish Roots: A Foundation of Biblical Theology for Messianic Judaism.* Pacific Palisades, Rockville: Davar Publishing Co., 1986.

Kac, Arthur. *The Spiritual Dilemma of the Jewish People.* Grand Rapids: Baker, 1983.

Kjaer-Hansen, Kai and Bodil F. Skjøtt. *Facts and Myths about the Messianic Congregations in Israel.* Jerusalem: Caspari Center, 1999.

Larsen, David L. *Jews, Gentiles and the Church.* Grand Rapids: Discovery House, 1995.

Loden, Lisa. "Issues Facing the Messianic Community in Israel Today." *LCJE Bulletin.* Arthus, Denmark, August 10, 2003.

Maoz, Baruch. *Judaism Is Not Jewish.* Ross-shire, Great Britain: Christian Focus Publications, Ltd., 2003.

Nichol, Richard C. "Messianic Judaism—So What Exactly Is It?' Messianic Jewish Life, Vol. LXXII, No. 3., July-Sept. 1999.

———. "So Ask the Rabbi." Messianic Jewish Life, Vol. LXXIII, No. 2., 1998.

Potok, Chaim. *Wanderings.* New York: Fawcett Crest, 1978.

Rausch, David A. *Messianic Judaism: Its History, Theology and Polity.* Lewiston, New York: The Edwin Mellen Press, 1982.

Roth, Cecil. *A History of the Marranos.* New York: Shocken, 1974.

Sachar, Abram Leon. *A History of the Jews.* New York: Alfred Knopf, 1965.

Sedaca, David. "Outreach through Messianic Jewish Congregations: A History and Insight for Today," *LCJE Bulletin.* Arthus, Denmark, May 2003.

Stern, David, H. *Messianic Jewish Manifesto*. Jerusalem, Israel: Jewish New Testament Publications, 1988.

Telchin, Stan. *Abandoned*. Grand Rapids: Chosen Books, 1997.

———. *Betrayed*. Grand Rapids. Chosen Books, 1982.

About Stan Telchin

For fourteen years Stan Telchin served as senior pastor of a church in Maryland made up of Jews and Gentiles from every walk of life, denomination, size and color. "We didn't concentrate on the things that divide," Stan says. "We concentrated on the One who unites. It was a loving, caring, wonderful church."

Stan has ministered in Canada, Iceland, Norway, Denmark, Finland, Ukraine, Russia, England, Germany and Israel. He has also been interviewed on scores of television and radio programs.

Perhaps Stan is best known for his very popular book *Betrayed*, which has been distributed in nations around the world. In it he describes how he set out to disprove the Messiahship of Jesus. But in trying to prove who Jesus was not, he learned who Jesus is.

He has also written *Abandoned: What Is God's Will for the Jewish People and the Church?* "*Betrayed* contains my story," Stan says, "but *Abandoned* contains my heart." In it he describes the underlying and very real issues that make it difficult for Jewish people to consider the Gospel. Then he provides important information to help motivate and equip the Church to reach out more effectively with God's love to their Jewish friends. He believes deeply that the message of this book needs to circle the globe.

Although an octogenarian, Stan is far from being retired. He now serves and continues to travel as a missionary with Jews for Jesus.

Here is how you can reach him:

Stan Telchin
6210 N. Lockwood Ridge Rd., #143
Sarasota, FL 34243-2529
stan@telchin.com
www.telchin.com

You can also contact him through:

Jews for Jesus
60 Haight St.
San Francisco, CA 94102

How do you feel when you are successful, 50 and Jewish, and your 21-year-old daughter tells you she believes in Jesus?

How do you feel when you are successful, 50 and Jewish, and your 21-year-old daughter tells you she believes in Jesus?

Betrayed!

Stan Telchin

Stan Telchin began his search through the Scriptures to find evidence to challenge the new faith his daughter had found in Jesus. Along the way, he faced personal challenges and revelations that demanded a life-changing decision.

Travel this road with Stan Telchin in the best-selling *Betrayed!* and discover
- a deeper, fuller awareness of Judaism and Christianity
- a healing attitude that can free you from the bitterness of the most heated conflicts and one family's resolution of a seemingly irreparable split

Has God *abandoned* the Jewish people?

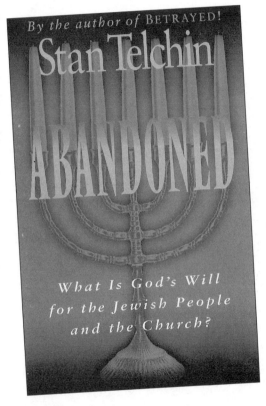

What do today's Jews believe about God and the Bible?

What keeps them from considering the Gospel?

Can you be Jewish *and* believe in Jesus?

Stan Telchin answers these questions and more in *Abandoned*, an invaluable guide for reaching out to the Jewish people. Telchin brings us right to the heart of the matter: why the Jewish people really need Jesus and how we can develop a faithful, loving witness to them.

Learn how to share God's love with the people who are always on His heart.